Productive Procrastination

Make it work *for* you,
not against you!

Kerul Kassel

Echelon Press, LLC

PRODUCTIVE PROCRASTINATION:
Make it work for you, not against you!
An Echelon Press Book

First Echelon Press paperback printing / January 2008

Echelon Press, LLC
9735 Country Meadows Lane 1-D
Laurel, MD 20723
www.echelonpress.com

ISBN 978-1-59080-546-6
Library of Congress Control Number: 2007933948

PRINTED IN THE UNITED STATES OF AMERICA

10 9 8 7 6 5 4 3 2 1   .

Acknowledgements

This book took considerably longer to publish than I expected. Indeed, I wrote and published a second book before this one saw print. It was a long path, and I have so many to thank for inspiring me, keeping me moving, holding me accountable, and providing an encouraging nudge forward.

Thank you to my mom and dad for providing a good example, whether or not I followed it. I am indebted to my mom, a true anticrastinator, my everlasting appreciation for the many and varied ways you've offered an abundance of support and guidance through the years. Your continued example of persistence, prolific activity, non-stop energy, and can-do attitude are still my role model.

To my husband Dave, my ongoing gratitude for your abiding affection, regard, thoughtfulness, and patience. Your relaxed and considered attitude about achieving goals has given me so much insight, helped me aid my clients, and informed the way I interact with them. Thank you for your unconditional love that has meant so much to me.

To my many colleagues for providing a sounding board, resources, perspective, reassurance, cheerleading, and so much more: Maria Andreu, Barbra Sundquist, Donna Steinhorn, Patricia Soldati, Sarah Dolliver, Carol Kauffman, Susan Meyer, Lynn Cohen, Marcia Merrill, Alix von Cramon, Judy Toth, and John Mitchell. Thank you for playing with me, challenging me, and helping me celebrate my successes.

To my publisher, Karen Syed, and her team for their confidence in me, their author-friendly business model, and their willingness to be flexible. You guys rock!

To my highly-valued and skilled proofreading team, for the amazing contribution you've made: Connie Frey, Julie Fleming-Brown, Coen de Groot, Maureen Coleman, and Vickie Turley. I will never forget your devoted assistance and high standards.

To my clients for being a continual source of insight, ideas, and stories; your courage and wisdom never fail to amaze me.

To my many teachers for pushing me (whether I wanted it or not), offering a new paradigm, and helping to equip me with the most effective tools available.

And to all you readers, for your dedication to your own improvement, your open minds, and your willingness to experiment with radical strategies. Without you, this book would still be just an idea.

Table of Contents

Introduction

Part I: *Procrastination Celebration*

Chapter 1: Let Go of Those Limiting Labels **11**

Chapter 2: Procrastinating for Success **29**

Chapter 3: Stop "Shoulding" on Yourself **43**

Chapter 4: Watched Pots and Your Best Instincts **63**

Chapter 5: The Importance of What's Important **81**

Chapter 6: Ready, Set, Wait **107**

Part II: *Procrastination Identification*

Chapter 7: When Procrastination Affects You **121**

Chapter 8: When Procrastination Affects Others **137**

Part III: *Procrastination Elimination*

Chapter 9: It's Real, It's Ugly...Now What? **153**

Chapter 10: Slaying the Inner Dragon **165**

Chapter 11: Tapping into the Power of Inspiration **179**

Chapter 12: Giving Yourself an Extra Edge **197**

Part IV: *Procrastination Organization*

Chapter 13: A Few Words About Managing Procrastination
in Your Business and Your Organization **215**

Part V: *The Procrastination Diary* **223**

Bibliography **285**

Introduction

"Anyone can do any amount of work provided it isn't the work he's supposed to be doing at the moment."

—Robert Benchley

Would you rather eat a live worm than file that pile of papers on your desk? Might you almost prefer to have a tooth drilled than start on that project you've been avoiding? (Let's not even talk, yet, about making that long-delayed dental appointment!)

How relieved would you be if I told you that you can feel GOOD about approximately half the instances in which you believe you're procrastinating?

That's right, no more self-recriminations, no more hair shirts, no more feeling like a slacker because you haven't gotten to (fill in the blank). How much does that really help you get things done, anyway?

The plain truth is that we all have a whole lot more that we need to do (not to mention what we'd *like* to do) than we have time for. There is no way we can complete all our plans, projects, responsibilities, and obligations, simply because we have far too many of them for 24 hours a day, 365 days a year (thank goodness for leap year…and its extra day!)

This means we need to concentrate on planning and completing those items that are the most important to us, that have the greatest ramifications on our ability to feel successful, capable, accomplished, and fulfilled.

The result is that we'd be better served by "productively procrastinating" on many of the tasks and projects we've been putting off. What a great idea!

In these pages you'll find some welcome liberation from the belief that you have to do everything, all the time, and perfectly at that. The first section of this book focuses on determining where procrastination might *not* really be happening, where you're successfully engaging in productive procrastination, and how to tell the difference between productive and destructive procrastination.

The second section describes a number of relatively simple, easy, and successful ways to motivate yourself to get started on and complete those important things you really **are** procrastinating on. Play with these, experiment, and don't stop trying until you're successful at it.

The third section describes a number of relatively simple, easy, and successful ways to motivate yourself to get started on and complete those important things you really **are** procrastinating (destructively) on.

When all is said and done, procrastination is really just a head game, a matter of attitude and perspective. We can persuade ourselves that the task is too large, onerous, and painful, or we can see the task as a brief challenge on our path to reaching the achievement

This book is based on my work with hundreds of people who have identified procrastination as the habit that holds them back from some of the success and happiness they desire. It has been written for those people I typically work with: those who are already doing a lot, but feel overwhelmed by the unending onslaught of "more to do."

Here's a caution: FOR SEVERE, RECALCITRANT, OR DANGEROUS CASES OF PROCRASTINATION, PLEASE CONSULT A THERAPIST OR OTHER MENTAL HEALTH PROFESSIONAL.

Part I:

Procrastination Celebration

Chapter 1
Let Go of Those Limiting Labels

Have you been putting things off? Are you stressed out and anxious on an everyday basis, just trying to keep up (forget even thinking about pursuing things you'd love to do)? Do you have a sense that you're not measuring up, and you're feeling a little out of control?

Yeah, you and everyone else!

Is the life you're living the one you really want for yourself? Is procrastination getting in the way? Whether you're a veteran procrastinator, or you just get stuck in certain places over and over, you'll be glad you've picked up this book. I'm keeping it short and sweet because, after all, how long does it take a procrastinator to finish reading a 500-page book on procrastination? Forever!

Let's reduce much of the stigma, pressure, judgment, and self-criticism of procrastination right off the bat, because once you start doing this your ability to deal with costly procrastination is much improved. We'll begin by examining the labels we've come to believe about ourselves in relation to procrastination, and by identifying what you're already doing well. We'll also slash your task list so you don't feel so overburdened, since it's likely that more than half of what's on your list you can forget about, at least for the moment. By peeling back the layers of desire, belief, intention, and commitment to see what really lies beneath, you'll be pleasantly surprised to find you're not such a slacker after all!

What the dictionary says

If you've been procrastinating long enough, it's likely that you already know that the word "procrastinate" comes from Latin. *Pro* (forward) + *crastinus* (belonging to the morrow)...and that's pretty interesting, isn't it? If it really belongs to the morrow, why on earth would we want to deal with it today?!

Webster's New World Dictionary of the English Language defines procrastinate as "to put off doing something until a future time; postpone or defer taking action." Notice that there's no judgment in the definition. Cool!

Now bear with me here.

We'll be covering not only how to use procrastination in a way that *benefits* you, but also:

- how to separate the good kind from the bad kind
- how to overcome the bad kind

Some things you should know about procrastination:

First: it's common!

Research indicates that 50-60% of adults surveyed reported that procrastination was an important problem for them, and 40% reported that procrastination cost them money. Women and men procrastinate pretty equally.

Thus far, there's no documented link between gender difference and frequency or severity of procrastination. One study indicated that procrastination peaks in men in the mid-to-late 20's, then declines over the next forty years, but increases again around age sixty. In women, it peaks around age twenty-five, declines until age fifty-five and then increases (but in later years is more increased for women than men).

Procrastinators are not stupid, either. No study has suggested that procrastinators are less intelligent than anyone else. My own survey indicates that over 35% of people who procrastinate have advanced college degrees.

It's not surprising that most studies of self-esteem in relation to procrastination show that they are interconnected. People with low self-esteem seem to be constantly critical of their performance. Of course, you could have high self-esteem in some areas (certain skills or talents, for example), and low self-esteem in others (appearance or intelligence, perhaps).

It seems that the more self-critical you are, the less likely you'll take risks, face anxiety, or accept challenges. A 1995 study found a strong relationship between conscientiousness and procrastination—in other words, the more meticulous you are, the harder your tasks seem to accomplish, and the more likely you are to put those tasks off. It also found that procrastinators have a low tolerance for frustration and difficulty delaying gratification. Kind of obvious, isn't it?

But even if you're a sixty-two-year-old man with low self-esteem about your ability to deal with details, or a forty-year-old woman who hates taking risks, or a twenty-four-year-old female doctoral student who is shy and retiring (even though very conscientious), or anyone else, for that matter, this book can help. It's not hard to stop procrastinating!

What the researchers say

M. Susan Roberts, Ph.D., author of *Living Without Procrastination,* defines procrastination like this: "When a task has value to you and your behavior does not follow, procrastination is occurring." Psychologists Albert Ellis and William Knaus define procrastination as "delaying task completion to the point of experiencing subjective discomfort."

Piers Steel, a professor and procrastination researcher at the University of Calgary, defines procrastination as "To voluntarily delay an intended course of action despite expecting to be worse off for the delay."

We can already see that procrastination hurts. But here's why you shouldn't beat yourself up so much:

Richard Swenson, M.D., author of *Margin: Restoring Emotional, Physical, Financial, and Time Reserves to Overloaded Lives,* attributes procrastination to overload, and lists the types of overloads he's observed:

Activity overload	Decision
Change overload	Education
Choice	Expectation
Commitment	Fatigue
Competition	Hurry
Debt	Information

Media	Problem
Ministry	Technology
Noise	Traffic
People	Waste
Pollution	Work
Possession	

Learning about this research is interesting, perhaps even somewhat enlightening, but by now you might begin to see…

It's what is behind procrastination that's more important.

When we focus on procrastination, we're actually only focusing on the outcome of *something that's occurring inside of us.*

So, here's my definition:

Procrastination is the product of conflicting objectives, desires, or beliefs.

Sometimes the conflicting objectives are between long-term goals and short-term rewards. There are the bright, shiny, visions of best-laid plans vs. the sexy, alluring siren's call of the in-the-moment impulse. It's much more appealing to go to the beach (short-term) than hunt out our receipts for tax return preparation (long-term), isn't it? We may want to be fit and slender (long-term), but right now that piece of cake (short-term!) is calling our name ever so seductively.

I'll bet you're getting the hang of this.

Let me introduce you to Chet and Amelia, two clients who illustrate this concept. Their stories, and those of others, will help you understand in practical terms the concepts I'm explaining. You may immediately recognize their inner conflicts and how those conflicting objectives result in procrastination behaviors.

Chet, a software entrepreneur with a thriving company, contacted me because, although he was financially successful, he felt like a slave to his business and a ghost to his family. He worked eighteen-hour days from home, rarely spent time with his children, did little to help his wife, and could see the toll it was taking. His wife was unhappy, and he could see his kids growing up fast without his involvement in their lives.

His software enterprise was so all-consuming, Chet felt unable to go on vacation or even take day a day off because he was worried that his business would fall apart. It was the kind of business, he believed, that always needed someone at the helm, 24/7/365. He didn't trust anyone else to handle the organization's affairs, and he was beginning to feel burned out. He had high standards, which had served him well, and which were, he believed, a big part of his identity.

Chet had begun to invest in some resort real estate to provide some passive income, but he was finding that it required more time and energy than he had anticipated. Things were getting worse, not better.

He had wanted to make some positive changes for some time, but he'd been putting off doing anything about the problem because he couldn't figure out where to start and what to do.

Amelia was also going through a rough patch. Her

mother had died last year after a long illness, and Amelia had been her caregiver during the whole time. She'd inherited a bit of money from her mother's estate, but it had been spent and now she had no job and no real direction. Yet, she kept putting off doing anything, despite feeling desperate.

Amelia lived with her fiancé, Edward, whose clutter had begun to annoy and depress her. She said that a medical condition prevented him from working, and he depended on her for expenses. The relationship left much to be desired in a number of other ways as well. Yet, she loved him, and believed he was a kind person with many good qualities. Also, she worried about how he would manage without her.

Amelia and Edward were planning to move from his apartment in the suburbs to the country. The house was in a rural area, and she was concerned that the location might affect her ability to make money.

Amelia also had a beautiful little studio apartment in the city that was vacant. She thought about selling it, but wondered if it was a good investment to hang onto despite the large mortgage. It was also an escape option if things didn't work out with Edward.

To generate some income and alleviate her financial crunch she had recently been thinking about creating a number of different business ventures, though she hadn't committed to any of them. She'd also thought of taking a part-time job in a school, but hadn't pursued it yet. If she was going to be moving, why bother?

Chet and Amelia both found themselves in

uncomfortable situations. They wanted positive change, but were delaying. There were not only costs for staying in their situation; there were payoffs for staying there, too. They didn't have to face possible unpleasant changes or risk unknown outcomes.

Sometimes the short-term reward really doesn't seem very rewarding.

Guess what? It is. The reward is that we don't have to deal with the thing that we're dreading!

That's why you clean the bathroom and organize your closet instead of evaluating your finances. It's why you might be having lots of dramas going on in your life that drain your energy. If you're too drained, you have a great excuse for avoiding that issue you *really* need to address.

Often, there are self-criticisms that are in conflict with our objectives. You'd like to write a book, perhaps, and you've got some really great ideas. When you sit in front of the computer, though, you soon find yourself doing something else, or not coming up with anything except self-disparaging thoughts. "What makes you think you can be a writer?" whirls around in your head and clouds your focus. I have plenty of experience in that area!

Sometimes we're aware of our conflicting commitments, beliefs, or intentions, and sometimes it takes some digging. Frequently, the obvious explanation gives us only a superficial understanding of what's really going on under the surface.

Chloe wants to write a book, but it's not happening. She offers lots of excuses. She's been busy with this, that, or some other thing, and every time she sits down to do it she gets interrupted. When I tell her that these were just convenient rationalizations for what she really felt, she is at first offended.

You know what they say, "The truth will set you free. But it might really piss you off, first." Once Chloe gets over her initial reaction, I ask her what uncomfortable thing might happen if she completes and publishes her book. It dawns on her that the real reason she resists writing is she might make a close friend uncomfortable, provoking too much pain to continue their friendship. This friend, she explains, has experienced some recent demoralizing failures in the publishing world. Chloe treasures the relationship and doesn't want to jeopardize it.

Above all, procrastination is caused by our resistance to, and avoidance of, feelings that occur in us, based on beliefs about how we think we need to be. It's both very simple and at the same time a bit deeper than we might expect. The case studies I'm including will illustrate how this works.

It's really helpful to understand that procrastination is simply the result of inner conflict.

Understanding what that conflict is may sometimes be straightforward, but at other times there may be less obvious reasons.

If, for example, you're not pursuing success as wholeheartedly as you think you should, you may not realize that it's because you're afraid that your family and friends, who are your primary support system, might resent your success. This seems reason enough to procrastinate, right?

Think about it: you're not being blocked because you're incapable, but because of your fear of the feelings of loss and rejection. This could feel devastating. On some level you might worry that those feelings will overwhelm you and you won't be able to cope. This fear of being overwhelmed is the common denominator behind *all* procrastination.

Fear, loathing, and overwhelm

You've had decades of training: every time something comes up that provokes a sense of discomfort, tension, or dread, there is the fear of overwhelm at the root of it.

You believe you ought to make phone calls to prospects to increase your business, and the specter of rejection looms. You look at your clutter and want to tackle it, but it looks like a mountain. You'd like to lose weight and become more fit, but when you consider the diet and required exercise, you just want to go take a nap.

If you probe a little more deeply, in every case where procrastination is going on, you'll see that, at the root, there is always a threat to your inner security: the fear of feeling overwhelmed.

It's ironic, but *the fear* of being overwhelmed by those feelings is much worse—is more draining and has more power to block your success—than the actual fears themselves. We're not even aware it's there, as we've become oblivious to it, but we do sense that we will be lost, destroyed, or overcome if we allow ourselves to "go there." And it's an illusion that "going there" will be scary or awful.

There's a distinction I'd like to make between feelings and emotions that will be helpful here. In common usage they are interchangeable, but they aren't the same. There are many psychological theories regarding emotions, but for the purposes of understanding procrastination, there is a difference I've found to be both simple and practical.

Feelings are sensations. They are the immediate energy that results from our sensory input (such as seeing, hearing, touching, tasting, and smelling, for instance). Did you know that there are more senses we have at our disposal than the traditional five? Intuition is a kind of sense that we're generally not aware of, and have mostly learned to discount. It is related to our somatic (bodily) or "visceral" response. It's how we feel in our gut (visceral is Latin for intestine), our heart, or even in our neck about things that happen to us (I'll be explaining more about this in Chapter 4.)

Emotions are mental constructs. They are stories that we create to understand what we are experiencing. We're constantly generating intellectual explanations based on patterns we've come to recognize, as well as the consequences we've experienced from those patterns. For example, let's say that as a kid your room was always in chaos and your parents constantly tried every method in the book to get you to clean it up. You lost privileges as a punishment. You were labeled "disorganized" or "lazy."

Although you probably built up a lot of resistance to being neat, as a result of all of the battles ("I gotta be me!"), at the same time you felt bad about not being "good" ("My resistance is costing me love").

Shift the scene to a decade or so later: any time your environment got out of control, those old emotions would recycle. You would remember that label: you're disorganized and lazy (loss of love). And that resentment would recycle too ("I am who I am").

Feelings are a direct result of sensory level data, and you experience them on a more physical, bodily level; emotions are our reaction to that data or to the feelings that follow. Both feelings and emotions occur in milliseconds, and they can seem intertwined. You could say there is a difference between what you "know" (feel or sense) about something, and what you "think" (emote or create a story in your head) about it. Perhaps whenever you look at clutter, there's a sinking feeling in your stomach, or tension in your shoulders that you don't even notice.

Both feelings and emotions are normal, valid, and also essential! They pass through us, just like the energy waves that they are. When you get stuck in them or, more precisely, stuck in *resisting* experiencing them, that's when they become limiting. That's when they have the power to cause you to procrastinate.

This distinction between feelings and emotions is useful, because resolving a procrastination block involves experiencing the one (feelings) without getting distracted by the other (emotions).

I mentioned earlier that we're generally not aware of our feelings. As infants, we are easily overcome by feelings and emotions, but we haven't yet learned to distinguish between the two. This is because we haven't yet developed the physical apparatus to handle large or complex feelings and emotions. Our physical apparatus for processing emotion is the spindle cell, a brain cell that collects information from one region of the brain and sends it on to other regions. It functions like an air traffic controller for emotions, and we have thousands of them.

When we're born, we don't have many spindle cells in our brains, but as we grow, we develop them, and our ability to process more intense emotions grows. You've seen the meltdowns that children sometimes have when they can't have what they want. It feels like the world is coming to an end for them. They simply haven't yet grown enough spindle cells to cope with the strength of the feeling they're experiencing. They are in a state of overwhelm, and it feels crushing.

As we grow, even though our capacity to manage our responses expands (we grow more spindle cells), we're still beleaguered with this sense of wanting to avoid those awful sensations we remember from our past experiences. It's a habit, and avoid it we do, as much as is possible.

Procrastination is a direct result of this avoidance.

Notice, however: you are not really avoiding being overwhelmed. You are avoiding the fear of it, because when you were very young, it felt awful. It's simply a patterned reaction we've all developed very early in life. We don't even recognize we're doing it.

You may have used discipline and willpower to overcome your worst moments in the past; this works, but it takes a lot of energy. A more effective approach is to peel back the layers to uncover what's underneath your foot-dragging ways, accept what's there, and move on.

The second half of this book focuses on simple techniques you can use to deal with situations in your life where procrastination is taking a toll. For now, let's take a look at some of the commitments (beliefs), in the form of labels, that you've accepted about yourself, and discover how you might already be using procrastination productively.

Where to begin?

Okay, admit it! You're a procrastinator, a loser. There's something you need to do and you're not doing it. You put stuff off until the last minute. With some things, at least, you can't get it together. You've tried before, and you can never seem to overcome this procrastination thing. You drag your feet, postpone, delay, put off, dawdle, loiter, dilly-dally, defer, hold off, let slide, tarry, and otherwise simply don't get certain things done. You feel at least a bit out of control and there's a sense that you don't have what it takes to cut the mustard.

Now, are you feeling effective and productive? Did that last paragraph inspire you to want to tackle those tasks, chores, and projects you've been ignoring? Are you all revved up and ready to conquer the world?

Probably not.

How does it affect you when you label yourself a procrastinator (and all the other stuff that comes with it)? Take a moment to really notice this. An immensely helpful (and empowering) first step is to be aware of your negative labels and then to start letting them go.

You've already received lots of feedback that putting

things off is not a good thing. More than that, though, it wasn't simply your behavior that was negatively judged. Your character was judged too. *You* were found lacking in some crucial way. These messages were intended to cause you to change your behavior, and generally they weren't complimentary.

What were those messages?

If your habit of postponing things goes back to childhood or adolescence, did your parents' nagging inspire you to be more proactive? It's doubtful. The techniques they used to get you to cooperate may have coerced you, pushed you, and strong armed you, but they were probably met with resistance on your part. Or perhaps you tried to be good, wanted to placate, and said you would comply, but then you forgot or got involved in other things, and didn't do what you were supposed to.

It's likely that your parents, or later, your teachers, other family members, authority figures and peers then started creating a story about who you are, which you "bought into" over time, and this has colored the way you conduct yourself in many areas in life. The labels then become self-fulfilling, and we eventually forget that we have a choice about how we want to function, and instead think "that's just who I am."

Mini-exercise

Take a moment to list the less-than-empowering labels that you've come to believe about yourself:

_____

_____

_____

Who gave you those labels?

_____

_____

_____

What evidence/experience do you have that makes those labels untrue? If you have difficulty coming up with some, look at various areas in your life where you may not be procrastinating, such as in work or home responsibilities, parenting or financial duties, favorite activities, or volunteer positions. If you think it will be helpful, ask your friends and family members for evidence.

_____

_____

_____

Here are the labels most commonly mentioned in my Procrastination Survey, in order of most frequently mentioned: lazy, slacker, loser, slob, scatter-brained, disorganized, undisciplined, stupid, and (not surprisingly) procrastinator.

Examining the labels you've accepted about yourself, particularly where they apply to a behavior like procrastination, is the beginning of the end for this problem and a vital step in a positive direction. Understand where and how you came to perceive yourself as a foot dragger. This gives you a choice about whether you want to continue living within the confines of those patterns.

I want to be clear: the purpose is *not* to heap blame on your parents, siblings, teachers, or others. They were doing the best they could. They were programmed with certain beliefs and values just like you. This exploration is not about trying to justify yourself as a victim, or to be absolved of personal responsibility for how you live your life.

In fact, exploring your labels should accomplish just the opposite. By observing how these false self-perceptions developed, you will more easily be able to drop the yoke of invalidation that robs you of energy.

Knowledge is Power! Even though you might still be procrastinating, you'll no longer be able to say, "That's just who I am." Now, you own what comes next. You'll be able to say, "This is who I've chosen to be."

Of course, I hope you'll choose a more satisfying

path! To help you make that choice, there are other factors to consider. In the next chapter, you'll read more about a new slant on procrastination, one that may release you from its dragging grip.

Let's examine the question of whether you're really procrastinating...or not!

Chapter 2:
Procrastinating for Success

"One of the greatest labor-saving inventions of today is tomorrow."

—Vincent T. Fos

When done properly, there really is a beautiful side to procrastination. I call that Productive Procrastination. Isn't that a freeing thought? Included in this heading are many of those things on your to-do list that aren't getting done. In this section, we'll discuss a number of reasons why some those to-do's *should* be postponed, and how procrastination might not really be what's going on with some of the others.

Here's a little secret. The most successful people procrastinate productively all the time. It's true!

Productive procrastination is…are you ready…the same thing as *effective time management*!

Are you a super-hero?

After all, you only have 24/7/365 (except for Leap year, and you're probably just giddy with anticipation over an additional twenty-four hours, aren't you?). There's only so much you can pack into that time. You can "have it all," but you just might not be able to have it all at once.

Compare your life to what it was like fifteen or twenty years ago. Didn't it seem a lot less complicated? Wasn't there considerably less pressure to be buff, beautiful, smart, sexy, successful, wealthy, and wise than there is today? There were fewer obligations, demands on your time, or multi-layered burdens of expectations. In this 21st century, we are blessed with a vast multitude of conveniences, opportunities, events to attend, subjects to learn, organizations to participate in, and other choices of many varied kinds. Indeed, there is such an overabundance of them that we end up feeling more stressed than blessed!

There is simply no precedent in the history of species *Homo sapiens* for dealing with this amount of complexity, information, and choice. It's understandable that many of us end up procrastinating, whether productively or destructively, as we wend our way through which long distance, and/or regional, and/or cellular provider to sign up for, after which we then have to consider each provider's multiple plans.

An exercise in modern complexity

Let's have a little fun with insurance, shall we? The purpose of this fun is to provide an example of the complexity, information, and choice we're faced with in every day life. When making insurance decisions, we have many categories to consider: automobile, health, homeowners or tenants, life, disability, liability, business, travel, extended warranty, and long-term care are what most people need. Here's a list of the categories provided by *one* insurance broker I found on the internet:

- Auto
- Fire & Theft
- Crime
- Antique & Classic Auto
- Umbrella
- Collateral
- Recreational Vehicle
- Earthquake
- Malpractice
- Motorcycle
- Flood
- Pets
- ATV & Snowmobile
- Life
- Equine & Livestock
- Warranty & Breakdown
- Estate & Retirement
- Church
- SR-22
- Annuities
- Aircraft
- Truck
- IRA's
- Whitewater
- Longhaul
- Securities
- Marine
- Boat
- Health
- Cargo
- Yacht
- Disability
- Bonds
- Watercraft
- Long Term Care
- Home
- Individual & Groups
- Condo
- Travel
- Apartment
- Business
- Mobile Home
- Mortgage
- Commercial
- Renters
- Retail
- Farm
- Contractors
- Growers
- Artisans
- Ranchers
- Manufacturers

Within the category of life insurance alone, there are five common types of insurance: term, whole, universal, variable, and variable universal. And then there are other types of life insurance, outside of these.

Health insurance decisions required you to pick from an HMO, a PPO, or a POS type of insurance provider.

When considering just auto insurance, these are choices you must make:

- Bodily Injury and Liability
- Car Rental
- Collision
- Comprehensive
- Credit Insurance
- Full Glass
- Gap Insurance (Leasing Only)
- Liability
- Medical Coverage
- No-Fault Insurance
- Out-of-Country Coverage
- Towing
- Personal Injury Protection (PIP)
- Underinsured or Uninsured Motorist

Each type of insurance has deductibles, co-pays, various exclusions, out-of-pocket maximums, policy limits, and more variables that have to be decided upon.

It's enough to make your head spin! You probably need a drink, or a nap, or a vacation, after just reading all of that.

And that's just on the topic of insurance!

It's not an excuse

Now, of course, I'm not suggesting that you procrastinate, even productively, on making certain that you're appropriately insured. I'm simply pointing out that it's very easy to allow yourself to become overwhelmed by what you need to know about and decide upon in just this one small area of modern life.

When you're overwhelmed, are you feeling productive and on top of things? Does it compel and motivate you into immediate and vigorous action? Does it elicit that sense of being energetically in control of your life?

Not exactly, right?

Unless you're willing to go out into the wilds and become a self-sufficient (and under-insured) hermit, it's very likely you're going to have to deal with a lot of details. And it's also quite probable that making informed decisions and acting on many of those details are not what you'd call "following your bliss." Yet, many of them still need to be done.

What you really need to know is that you're not lazy, bad, or unworthy because you don't get everything done on time. While we've all been given many messages that imply exactly that, it's simply *not true*! It's a sure bet that you've already made significant contributions to your friends, your family, your colleagues, your industry, and the world at large, whether by supporting or caring for others, providing useful information and/or valuable services, or even asking questions that resulted in some benefit being created to someone or something.

Many books and cultural notions these days place an emphasis on doing something "big" in the world. This puts a lot of pressure on us. We can't all be Mother Teresa, Martin Luther King, or Jane Goodall, nor should we feel compelled to have to do something so visible and massive. The other side of this coin, though, is taking the examples of those icons to inspire us to contribute something of ourselves for the betterment of both the world and ourselves without letting these models daunt us.

We live in a world that places a huge emphasis and value on celebrity and fame, and much less value on less visible or less "sexy" contributions. If it isn't big and splashy, it doesn't feel like it's enough (and if it *is* big and splashy, it feels like it's *too* much). This puts us in a bind with few options. Much of overcoming procrastination involves recognizing that you have more plausible options than you currently think you do.

In Part III of this book, you'll find a number of concepts and strategies that will help you identify (or create) and then explore those options so that you can accomplish those tasks and responsibilities that are important and necessary but not inherently pleasant or enjoyable. For now, though, I'm sure you're eagerly anticipating reading more about...

Productive Procrastination

Not *all* of those things on your to-do list need to be completed in the very near future, and some of them *never* need to be done! I'd just about guarantee it! I've worked with hundreds of people, just about everyone of whom could shred close to half of their to-do's.

It's precisely because there is so much to do, know, be, and have that it's in your best interests to productively procrastinate on those things that are not, in the grand overall scheme of your life, crucial.

I know what at least some of you are thinking…*everything* is important!

Peter was convinced that he was procrastinating about cleaning up his office clutter and that it was an issue that was important and needed attention. When asked, he felt strongly that he was at fault and was holding himself back in his business by not taking responsibility for the mess.

I asked Peter what he had done in the past, if anything. He said that he'd hired a woman occasionally to help him file and clean things up, but felt this was a cop out, as well as not being a sustainable method since he was just as cluttered a few weeks later. It was clear he was feeling badly about his lack of progress with this aspect of his business life, and it was affecting his self-image.

When I asked Peter what he was best at, he described his ample business talents. Then I asked him whether organizing papers was included among those talents. Not surprisingly, the answer was "no." Finally, I asked whether filing and paper management tasks were the best use of his time and talents, or whether he'd gain more by utilizing his own gifts, and regularly paying someone else to utilize their talents to keep his office organized and clutter-free.

Once the situation was reframed, Peter was able to understand that his commitment to having an uncluttered office was in conflict with his commitment to the belief that he needed to do it himself. Now that the competing commitment was uncovered, it was clear to him that his desire to have an organized workspace was stronger than an unreasonable dedication to doing everything himself.

By the end of our conversation he was no longer opposed to the idea of hiring someone to regularly file and manage his paperwork; indeed, he was now eagerly looking forward to it. He was now free to devote more time and energy to running his business rather than allowing that energy to be lessened by the specific self-criticism that he wasn't capable of handling his clutter, and the general self-criticism that he therefore didn't have control of himself.

Second-guessing how you spend your time

Personally, while I've gotten pretty good about overcoming procrastination, it's been a journey, one that I find I'm still traveling on occasion. For me, the "everything is important" syndrome is particularly resonant. Like so many of my clients, in spite of having the knowledge about how to prioritize and plan and schedule, I still occasionally find myself doubting that whatever I'm doing in any moment is the right thing to be doing. At those times, no matter what I'm doing, I think I should be doing something else. While I'm writing in this book, my thoughts wander: should I be reading some industry journals, or checking and replying to my ever-increasing emails? And shouldn't I call back my in-laws who called yesterday (because morning is the best time to reach them)? But what about putting up the holiday decorations, which I've been meaning to do for the last week? Or preparing the bank deposits that need to get to the bank today, or making sure the tax collector has received my real estate tax check, or calling an organization that sent me some contracts that need changing, not to mention buying holiday gifts for my extended family (it's about three weeks until Christmas at the moment)?

Of course, I've already scheduled much of that stuff into my calendar and am pretty dependable about getting to it, and I approach my life with a sense of experimentation that allows for greater flexibility. Yet, I still find that as productive and planned and details-dealt-with a life as I've created for myself, as much as I've delegated and simplified, there's still that nagging sense that I'm not doing the right or important thing at certain moments. I catch myself in a pattern of doubting my ability to do things right or at the right time, or to get everything done that I've identified as important.

I've come to recognize that in the past I've allowed that doubt to drain my confidence, energy, and effectiveness but I've learned that I can use the doubt more successfully as a check and balance (rather than a self-criticism) to keep myself on track.

In my experience, when everything seems important, and it's hard to prioritize, this simply indicates a momentary sense of overwhelm. Take a deep breath and a closer look. Perhaps a simple prioritization system is needed (see Chapter 5), or perfectionist tendencies might be recognized, accepted, and let go of (see Chapter 6). But before we explore that, a little groundwork is called for.

Intentions, objectives, goals, and tasks

While you may think of goals and objectives as synonymous with each other, I define them differently. Objectives are longer-term, bigger picture desires, dreams, and accomplishments, whereas goals are stepping-stones along the way to those objectives. Tasks are the even smaller actions that lead to achieving goals. When coaching procrastinators, this is an important distinction, since breaking down objectives into lesser goals and even more granular tasks makes planning easier and reduces the overwhelm most people experience when aiming high or contemplating big projects or dreams— and sometimes smaller ones.

Now let's add the concept of intention into the mix. Intention is why you create the objective in the first place.

Here's an example to illustrate how these distinctions are helpful, using one of the top four items people have listed in my Procrastination Survey: getting organized. Getting organized is the objective, and the goals toward that objective could include getting rid of junk and clutter and putting what's left into some semblance of order, using systems that are sustainable so you can stay organized consistently. Tasks that would serve this goal could include; cleaning off your desk, sorting stuff, creating a new filing system, going through your files and throwing out "dead" files, putting some files into short or longer term storage, cleaning out your office, kitchen, bathroom, or garage cabinets and reorganizing them, creating a new system to deal with incoming mail, bills to be paid, reading materials that accumulate, etc. Okay, that's pretty obvious, right?

Intention is *why you want to* get organized. Getting and staying organized isn't something most people do because they have fun doing it (though some people do, believe it or not), but because they want the ease, peace of mind, ability to focus, and effectiveness that result from being able to find things easily and think more clearly, in a streamlined space. This is the motivation behind all organizing efforts, just as feeling good about yourself is one of the core motivations behind exercising, weight-loss, and getting-in-shape objectives.

Intention is important to explore because without doing so we often create objectives and goals that make it harder for us to achieve our intentions by limiting us to the one outcome we're looking for. Perhaps you think your closet has to look like a California Closets advertisement. And if it doesn't look as tidy and color-coordinated, if the hangers aren't all the same and an even inch apart, if you have many colors, different prints, red boots that don't fit into the shoe compartment, and a big floppy hat that doesn't fit anywhere, you think you've failed. Those ads, you see, are really just fantasy. Nobody's closet really looks like that, unless they wear only brown and blue, have only three pairs of jeans, four sweaters, and five pairs of shoes. But if you connect with what you really want—a closet where you can easily hang something, where things aren't falling over, where you can find what you're looking for, where you actually wear most of what's hung there—that's success.

Referring back to your intention gives you many more options and more flexibility. It also gives you more inspiration. If you think to yourself "I'm such a slob—I have to get more organized!" you're already at a disadvantage. However, if instead you refer to what motivates you—peace of mind and effectiveness, for example—that's a lot more appealing and has much more sustainability. We'll delve deeper into exploring and experimenting with intentions and options in Chapter 11.

How could it be possibly be productive?

There are three essential ways that you might be productively procrastinating. When you look at your list of unaccomplished tasks and goals, upon closer inspection you might find some items will fit into any or all of the following categories:

It's not the right goal—
- it's not your goal; it's someone else's
- it's not worth pursuing
- there's a better or easier way to reach your intention

It's not the right time—
- you're not ready yet
- the opportunity isn't ripe enough

- the window of opportunity has already passed
- you have other, more important, priorities

You don't have all the information you need in order to continue—

- you're waiting for additional information from somewhere or someone before you can continue
- there's some vital internal question you haven't yet answered or decided
- you think you need to make "the right" decision, rather than the best decision based on the circumstances

Remember, I said "upon closer inspection." So bear with me a minute. I'm guessing you believe that nothing on your list falls into those categories.

Let's take a closer look, though, and see what you might be able to cross off your list.

Chapter 3
Stop "Shoulding" on Yourself

*"Never put off until tomorrow what you can do
the day after tomorrow."*

—Mark Twain

I hear it all the time. Oh, if I had even a penny for
every time I heard someone use the word "should" (as in
"I should really do the _____" or "I know I should finish
the ____" or "I should _____, shouldn't I?"), I'd be
vacationing for three months in Hawaii every year.

Ask yourself this: how does "should" feel? If you've
never examined this, take a minute now to give it some
thought. I'd be willing to bet bagels to buffalo nickels that
it doesn't feel GREAT. In fact, if you're willing to admit
it, "should" feels heavy, boring, and dull. Resistance is an
almost automatic reaction to the word "should." It's no
wonder you're putting things off!

That resistance or rebellion might be a holdover
reaction to your mother nagging you to clean your room
or finish your homework before you went out to play. Or
perhaps your summer camp counselor requiring you to
complete the craft project you were working on before
you started a new one, or some other long-ago seed that
was planted and has now grown into a huge
procrastination monster. The truth is, it's less important

how it got started, but only that you become aware that your current foot-dragging is most likely a relic of some childhood dynamic you're still acting out. Ouch! And you thought you were a grown-up!

For the heck of it, ask yourself how "want" feels? Quite a different picture, hmmm? "Want" is more about something you desire, some outcome you're inspired to reach for.

Almost any time you use the word "should" there's an implied "but don't wanna." Through my work I've found that many of my clients' "shoulds" fall under the category of productive procrastination.

Wouldn't it be great to "want" to do some of our "shoulds"? You'll be reading more about this in Chapter 11. For now, though, the key point to focus on is that "should" is a red flag. "Should" usually means it's something you don't really want to do but feel in some way duty-bound to accomplish. Let's take a closer look at "should."

A partial outline of Sheila's dissertation had been sitting on her desk, in plain view for months, as a reminder that she needed to work on it. More recently, it had gotten mixed into a three-inch pile of papers that had been building for another couple of months. Sheila had been trying to complete the requirements for her doctoral degree for the past two years. It was slow going, and life just seemed to be getting in the way. Each time she thought about the need to work on that dissertation, she felt the sharp pang of self-disapproval for not having already completed the work. Whenever a free evening presented itself, however, she always found "more important" things to do. The lack of movement on her dissertation seemed to bleed into the rest of her life, lending a feeling that she wasn't capable of finishing things, and it slowed her progress in her career, too.

Time marched on. After spending another year in this way, Sheila happened to attend a presentation on procrastination, during which she had an epiphany. The doctoral degree wasn't really something she wanted for herself. Her heart wasn't in it. It was a family expectation, and she wasn't even particularly interested in her area of study, but had just sort of accepted it as the path she was supposed to tread. No wonder she had such difficulty pushing herself! This revelation allowed her, for the first time, to question what it was she really did want. Having spent so many years unconsciously training herself away from it, it took some time to excavate those deeply buried interests and passions.

Do you know what *you* really want?

Please don't take this as a license to be irresponsible, lacking in integrity, insensitive, or egocentric—on the contrary. This is about being true to yourself, which includes doing those things that may not be particularly enjoyable or easy, but are still in line with how you (as a unique individual) need to operate to have the success, enjoyment, freedom, and peace of mind you want.

Once she'd examined her motivations Sheila might have chosen to continue with her dissertation, and it would have been a choice that was informed by what she truly wanted for herself. Or she might have chosen another direction, knowing that continuing to apply herself to an area in which she wasn't really interested would have led to a career that wasn't satisfying, fun, or fulfilling except for perhaps paying the bills, having those letters at the end of her name, and a sense of accomplishing something that was difficult (though not aligned with what she wanted). That might be enough for some people, but is it enough for you?

Most of us are not in the least aware that we're shoulding on ourselves. It's a revelation to realize how controlled we are by the perceptions of others, of our upbringing, and of our culture in such a constant and pervasive way.

In her book, "*Finding Your North Star*," Martha Beck presents the ideas of the "essential" self and the "social" self. The essential self is the part of you that knows the answers you're seeking, the preferences that make up who you really are, the compass that points toward the life that's rich, satisfying, and meant for you. The social self, on the other hand, is the side of you that has learned to value the things that others around you value. Very often it completely eclipses our essential selves, so much so that when someone asks us what really lights our bulb, it takes seven or eight social self answers before any of the essential self-ideas start to seep to the surface, if they're allowed any visibility at all.

Ask yourself whose voice it is that's playing on a tape in your head dictating the *should*. Is it your parents, siblings, teachers, bosses, religious leaders, or even the infamous "Everyone"? Your *Everyone* might include popular cultural norms, political or ideological groups, people you went to school with, your friends or even your enemies!

Once you realize that it's not your own vote, but someone else's, you can decide whether you want to continue to let socialite cousin Kate dictate that your bust and your hair color might be fake, but that your pearls and your silver must be real. Perhaps your long dead high school coach is making you work eighty-five hours a week, because he told you that if you *really* wanted to win, the only way is through constant, unflagging, undistracted, dogged dedication. Buying into that belief means that you will never be able to get what you want with ease, and it will be harder to enjoy, too.

You might ask yourself whether these others have the best and highest results in mind for you or if, instead, their possibly misguided efforts to influence you are to keep you in line, comfortable for them to relate to and feel aligned with. This is not to villainize anyone! I'm assuming well-intentioned and caring influences.

What I'd like you to take from this is the awareness that your dawdling might be due to the possibility that your goal isn't really yours after all. What goals, tasks, chores, projects, initiatives, or ambitions do you have that may not really be yours?

Mini-exercise

Things I'm shoulding on myself about:

_____

_____

_____

Now ask yourself the following questions about each "should" you've listed:

- Apart from what others think, and if they didn't care one way or the other about your doing this, would you want to do it?
- What choices do you truly have about it?
- How does this "should" stack up against other things you're pursuing for yourself, in terms of priority?
- What will doing this "should" cost you?
- What will not doing it cost you?

Changing your "should" perception

Sometimes "shoulds" are wants, and we procrastinate because we've developed a way of viewing certain chores, tasks, projects, work, or goals as having some negative attributes. Maybe we've come to see work as a necessary evil rather than as something that we want to do because it could be interesting, fun, or challenging in an enjoyable way. Or we put off dealing with clutter because it's hard, tedious, or mountainous instead of wanting to enjoy a system we've created to help us keep on top of things and stay organized. We've developed a conviction about how distasteful or grueling things are and pessimistic expectations about how our progress (or lack thereof!) will go.

In his book, *The Luck Factor*, Dr. Richard Wiseman describes how people who view the world pessimistically, and themselves as unlucky, think and act in ways that actually increase their bad luck, which adds to their negative outlook on life. They smiled less, were less likely to develop rapport and relationships with people they met, and were less likely to take advantage of opportunities. That's a vicious cycle. He also observed how people who perceived themselves as lucky thought and acted in ways that enhanced their luck—they were more open and accepting of others, acted on more opportunities, took more risks, and kept their sense of humor. What's even more interesting is that both groups had approximately the same number and types of mishaps, such as accidents, investments gone sour, illnesses, etc. For the self-considered lucky ones, these challenges were seen as temporary and leading to something better. The pessimists, on the other hand, used the challenges to confirm their world-view that life is hard, it's getting worse, and it's never going to get better.

Remember this whenever you find yourself being Negative Nelly.

Is what you have listed just a set of "shoulds" or are they "musts" or even "want to's" masquerading as "shoulds"? Refer to Part II to help you distinguish whether it's productive or destructive procrastination and Part III for how you might change a "should" back into a "want to."

Absolute Perfection

"You can spend a lifetime, and, if you're honest with yourself, never once was your work perfect."

—Charlton Heston

Ah, perfection. It's another way you should on yourself. Even though many people engage in perfectionism in a destructively procrastinating way, it is also sometimes a form of productive procrastination. In any case, since we're discussing "shoulds" in this chapter it's a perfectly opportune time to discuss aiming for perfection.

The word perfect can be defined in a number of ways. Mostly, we define perfection as the state of being ideal, without flaw or fault. The root, of course, is perfect. The dictionary defines perfect as:

1. Lacking nothing essential to the whole; complete of its nature or kind.
2. Being without defect or blemish: *a perfect specimen.*
3. Thoroughly skilled or talented in a certain field or area; proficient.
4. Completely suited for a particular purpose or situation: *She was the perfect actress for the part.*
5. Completely corresponding to a description, standard, or type: *a perfect circle; a perfect gentleman.*

      a. Accurately reproducing an original: *a perfect copy of the painting.*

6. Complete; thorough; utter: *a perfect fool.*
7. Pure; undiluted; unmixed: *perfect red.*
8. Excellent and delightful in all respects: *a perfect day.*

Mainly, we don't see perfection when we focus on what we see as obvious flaws, blemishes, or defects. There's a lot of pressure to be Number One, and for the most part we buy into it.

People who maintain high standards for themselves and others are more likely to spend much time and effort on perfecting something, but nobody is completely immune. In these days of reality television shows where there's only one winner and everyone else is considered losers, the force of that competitive value is held in ever-higher regard, and its seduction is increasingly tempting. That makes it harder for us to be more flexible about outcomes, and we lose our perspective. So, let's zoom out for a bit to get an aerial view of the forest, so we're not just looking at the trees.

The 80/20 Rule

The Pareto Principle, also known as the 80/20 Rule, states that a small number of causes (20%) are responsible for a large percentage (80%) of the effect.

Italian economist Vilfredo Pareto created a

mathematical formula to describe the unequal distribution of wealth in his country in 1906, observing that twenty percent of the people owned eighty percent of the wealth.

After Pareto made his observation and created his formula, many others observed similar phenomena in their own areas of expertise. Quality Management pioneer, Dr. Joseph Juran, working in the US in the 1930s and 40s, recognized a universal principle he called the "vital few and trivial many" and reduced it to writing.

That's when the principle that 20% of something is always responsible for 80% of the results became more commonly known as the 80/20 Rule.

And this 80/20 rule applies in so many instances.

Think about this: don't you use 20% of your wardrobe 80% of the time? How about foods in your pantry and refrigerator, or the kitchen gadgets in your cabinets, or the files in your file cabinet, or the books and magazines in your bookshelf, or the toiletries in your bathroom? It's likely you use 20% of the items 80% of the time, and the other 80% only 20% of the time.

Of the tasks you've got on your to-do list, there are probably 20% that are worthwhile spending 80% of your time on, and the other 80% are less of a priority and worth only 20% of your time, at least measuring by what you need to accomplish today.

Another way to apply this rule is to put effort into something until its 80% perfect and stop there. It may take you 80% more time to perfect the final 20% of the effort toward 100% perfect.

This reminds me of a colleague in the professional organizing business. Her business name is *Organized Enough*. Don't you just love that!

There is a point of diminishing returns, beyond which it becomes counterproductive to continue with any task. If you have a recognized tendency to be a perfectionist, I'm not suggesting you lower your standards drastically, but only enough to make it worthwhile and get it done. The reason for perfectionism is a fear of delayed failure. If you've put your all into achieving something, there's nothing left to muster if your efforts somehow don't measure up. If you've invested everything you have but it still doesn't meet with approval, or you're called upon to deliver in increasingly challenging responsibilities, the possibility of failure can be a real procrastination invitation.

Mediocre progress is superior to infinitely delayed perfection

You may know this is true, but are still resisting it. You've come to identify yourself as someone who has high standards, and others see you in this light as well. It may feel like a slippery slope to ease up on those standards. I'm not suggesting that you become sloppy or careless, far from it. There is a middle ground, or an above average ground, if that makes you feel more comfortable. I only recommend that you take a look at everything on your plate and evaluate where it really counts to maintain your standards, and where it makes sense to relax them a bit. Explore what it may be costing you to have to uphold a more rigorous benchmark.

Mini-exercise

List three tasks that you feel you can afford to stop at 80% of your original expectation:

1. _____

2. _____

3. _____

A job worth doing is worth doing well enough

I've seen it happen many times that a client has created a beautiful and "perfect" system, but it takes too much effort and inconvenience to maintain it so within a couple of weeks the system breaks down. If systems and habits are made too complex overwhelm can easily set in. The number and variety of everything we have to keep up with makes the small rigors of anything but a relatively simple system a candidate for procrastination.

But what if you were to take a more flexible attitude? What if well enough *were* enough? Sure, we've been taught that if it's not the most, top notch, Number One it's not worthy, but have you found that belief helpful and useful, and do you want to keep living under its unforgiving thumb?

Make no mistake; I'm not suggesting that you do less than your best. What if your best took into account the multitude, complexity, and difficulty of *everything* you had to accomplish, rather than just this one individual task?

Something else to consider if you've got perfectionist tendencies is how much you enjoy doing things to perfection. If you're really getting pleasure out of it, and there isn't something important and pressing that is being tabled or ignored, go for it! But if, instead, you feel dogged, grouchy, pressured, if your perfectionism is fear-based, you might want to develop a little more give in your attitude.

Another view of perfection

For some time now, I've been having my clients play with the idea that something is perfect simply because that's the way it's happened; that it's perfect because the universe (or substitute the God of your choice) permits or arranges things to develop in this way.

Thomas Leonard, the founder of the personal and business coaching industry, promoted the idea that perfection was not necessarily "ideal" in the typical sense, but instead ideal because there are powerful lessons or gifts in any situation, even if that situation seems far from perfect according to how we're used to defining the word. Rather than simply casting the situation in a negative light, how could you make the most of it? How could you use the circumstance to bring out your greatness? Here's an example:

Madeleine had been grappling with the demands of her own business and how they conflicted with the desire to be a good mother. For some time she had been feeling pretty badly that she enjoyed her business so much, but that it left little time and energy to spend with her children. Madeleine enjoyed her kids, but they were at the age where they required a lot of vigor and attention, and she found it difficult to summon this for them on a daily basis. Worse, it wasn't just her own inner critic voicing ideas about the amount and type of interaction that was called for; her kids were making more specific and strongly voiced demands to spend time with her.

At the core Madeleine's biggest concern was what it would mean about her if she didn't fit the "good mom" mold. Her own mother had made Madeleine a priority. As a child Madeleine was her mother's job. Madeleine's mom had left some big shoes to fill, and it strongly influenced her ideas of what it meant to be a good mother. She also wanted her children to grow up well adjusted, have happy lives, and not say hateful things about her mothering skills.

As altruistic as we believe we're being, the reason we have problems is still all about us, not someone else. I know, that's kind of a let down, isn't it? But it's true, nonetheless.

There were kid activities she was trying to fit into her schedule (but procrastinating with) that would fit the pattern of good mom, such as baking cookies with them, engaging them in elaborate crafts projects, and taking her kids to all sorts of lessons. But Madeleine had the self-awareness to know that she didn't enjoy those things and it was unlikely she would do them, at least not with consistency. She felt stuck.

We used a coaching technique that allowed her to experience and get past the uncomfortable sense of what she wasn't doing, and give her more perspective on how she could be the greatest mom she could be. When I asked what gifts or skills she had in that area, she mentioned her sense of humor, her candidness, and her ability to engage her kids in interesting conversations (when they weren't bouncing off the walls!). And perhaps she could use her natural networking abilities to put her in touch with others to find some resources and support that could help. Finally, when I asked her what might be perfect about the situation she found herself in, she replied that it propelled her to seek her own best-lived version of being a great mother rather than some never-achievable fantasy.

She wrote a little while later to give me an update:

"First, I got on IM right away and made an appointment to talk to Mark [a friend of hers who is a parent and is also a parenting coach] later in the day. Then I headed to a scheduled lunch with a colleague... AND my daughter. It was strictly a social thing, but not the type of thing I do (the "perfect professional" me would never lug a four-year-old to a chic lunch spot). And she was the perfect lady and had lunch with us. Then I spent the afternoon at the park with her. I have tons of stuff to write (but mercifully I had no classes or clients) but I spent the afternoon rollerblading and sitting on a bench eating ice cream and talking about the complexities of life as a four-year-old. And for this one afternoon, I was the perfect mom."

Madeleine had a website log, also known as a "blog" that she wrote in regularly. Her entry in the blog that day talked about how she understood that what she needed was to make this way of mothering sustainable. She acknowledged that there would be days where it would be much more trying than others; that her work might threaten to get in the way and that her children might be overly difficult or demanding. But she recognized that to achieve sustainability it was vital to set up supports in her life, so that those challenges would occur less frequently or in lower intensities, or be less of an obstacle to being the kind of good mom she wants to be. It wasn't about being a perfect mom, she realized. It was about creating the kind of life for herself where she provided for her own nurturance and stimulation, where she created space for her own brand of creativity and expression, and where she found companionship not only with her husband and children, but also amongst people that she admired, respected, and whose friendship stretched and expanded her. And that would also make her a more relaxed, tuned-in, and available mother. Madeleine was on her way to overthrowing perfection.

I'll cover more about environments in the third section of this book.

Mini-exercise

List three areas/roles/responsibilities/habits/tasks/ projects in which you're pursuing perfection, and might be willing to become somewhat more flexible:

1. _____

2. _____

3. _____

Chapter 4
Watched Pots and Your Best Instincts

You've been dragging your feet, hanging fire, and now you're going to exert some will power. You squeeze up the determination to get going and...WHAM. Dead stop.

You're stuck and feel you can't move forward. You start in with self-recrimination, and before you know it you're really in a pit of self-loathing and self-pity. Perhaps you'll pull out the blame game and start rationalizing who is at fault (other than you, of course) for your situation.

It's more than likely that within minutes, if not seconds, you'll move on to some other activity, one that will help you avoid this uncomfortable sensation, or at least put off feeling it for any longer.

Maybe you'll even do something else you've been procrastinating on so that you can feel better about not doing the task that you're really ducking. This is what Rita Emmett, author of *The Procrastinator's Handbook: Mastering the Art of Doing It Now* calls "noble procrastination." Ironic, and amusing, isn't it?

Sitting here right now, not knowing what is next for this page, I'm tempted to see if I have any new e-mail, to work on a different project, and/or go see what is in the refrigerator that might be appealing. If I finish composing a thought or concept, and another isn't immediately apparent, there's a pause. In that pause is where I am at first uncomfortable and then seek to avoid that discomfort by jumping to something less unpleasant. I must persistently retrain my focus on continuing, to make the choice to be present to this task rather than allowing myself to be swayed by the impulse to do "Anything but this!"

And that takes less self-discipline than you might imagine, incredibly! Look for more detail on this in Part II of this book.

There are many rather obvious reasons for putting something off. Here are a few possibilities:

FEARS

Fear of failure
Fear of success
Fear of change
Fear of making a mistake
Fear of looking foolish
Fear of rejection
Fear of being imperfect
Fear of the unknown
Fear of having to compete against others
Fear of risk or of the outcome
Fear of having to live with our choice
Fear of giving up what we already have
Fear that you'll be neglecting other things

Fear that this will take too much time

CHALLENGES

Underdeveloped skill in delegating
Underdeveloped skill in saying no
Underdeveloped skill in prioritizing
Underdeveloped skill in accepting responsibility
Indecision
Underdeveloped confidence
Starting hurdle blues
Tedious, boring, or unpleasant tasks
Perfectionism
Enabled by others

Any of those resonate with you?

What does it look like when you're procrastinating? While these indicators and outcomes don't predict procrastination exclusively, if they are there it's likely that procrastination is a factor or indicator.

RESULTS AND INDICATORS OF PROCRASTINATION

Overwhelm
Exhaustion
Depression
Perceived lack of purpose or mission to task
Anxiety
Guilt
Stress

Illness or health is suffering
Low self-esteem
Shame
Feeling out of control
Having to pay late fees, finance charges
Clutter—shuffling through piles every day

Is that sufficiently depressing?

Well, here is another list of reasons why you might really be procrastinating, and these have a different focus, one that is designed to help foster awareness of how delaying on some of your tasks might be appropriate or even, (heavens!)…wise.

All of these reasons fall under the heading of "it's the wrong time."

1. You're not ready yet; you need to travel further along the path to get to the turnoff.

2. The opportunity isn't yet ripe, even though you don't consciously recognize it.

3. The window of opportunity has already passed.

4. Don't waste your time: there are other, more important, priorities.

Let's take a look at these in more detail.

You're not ready yet

Patty's friends are holding a workshop this weekend on creating seminars and workshops where the participants embody the learning. She thought it would be perfect because she wants to build the workshop piece of her business. It was being held by friends, and promised to deliver what she felt she needed. It was a real no-brainer for her.

But she has continually put off signing up for it. Of course, she also feels badly about not acting on it, and it reinforces her idea that she's a procrastinator. It breeds a sense of not being in control.

Once we more closely examined why she was delaying, she came to a realization. Instead of berating herself for postponing registration, she checked in with herself about why she hadn't signed up for the course. The outcome was that she realized that in her heart she knew it wasn't the right time. She's simply not ready for it yet. She has decided to not go to the workshop, and now she feels completely fine about not going.

For Patty, attending the workshop was a choice, not a necessity, and while it seemed important in the overall scheme of what she wanted, the timing was off for her to attend when this particular workshop was being offered. Before she had given it more consideration, it seemed like less of a choice to her, and appeared to be just another indication that she would never achieve her dreams and goals because she's a procrastinator.

If there is some goal or dream that you've had in mind for a while (and it's not a "should"), yet you feel like you're not really making progress toward it, there may be a few things happening.

No or slow?

It's possible you're making more progress than you think. My clients often complain that they're not making progress. They're frustrated, they feel stuck, and they worry that they'll never achieve what they desire. When I question them on what they're doing to pursue it, I may find that they are taking actions and having some progress. It's just not fast enough to suit them! They want to be "there" yesterday.

We all easily fall prey to this. We judge ourselves continually on how we haven't yet achieved our goals, not realizing how far we've really come.

Tina had been feeling discouraged and thwarted in her efforts to build her consulting business and leave her administrative job. She had been educating herself in the consulting industry and making some good connections, but there were certain business-building tasks that she was not doing as she believed she should. She was tired of her administrative position, even though it currently fit her lifestyle as she could work part time from home and be available for her children, but she ached to be done with it and move on to this more exciting new venture. Yet she needed the income from the job, as the consulting business wasn't yet profitable enough to support her. While her husband had a secure position, it wasn't enough to support the lifestyle that they had chosen.

Part of her goal in business was financial independence, and she felt that she would never get there.

Perspective is often elusive when you feel like you're in a dark tunnel and the light at the end does not yet seem visible. For Tina, it was a journal that provided that perspective. As a form of "noble" procrastination, rather than doing work on her business (or her job!), she decided to clean out some closets. In the process, she uncovered a journal from a few years earlier.

Written at a stressful time in her life, when she had a young child and a demanding full-time job, it contained a wish list of what she wanted her life to be like. She was amazed and delighted to realize that she had achieved every single goal on that list. She hadn't actively pursued these goals, and had forgotten she'd even written them down.

Without the benefit of seeing where she'd come from and where she currently was, the improvements she'd made in her life seemed invisible or non-existent. This reinforced the notion that she'd never get what she wanted. It kept her disheartened and in a state of struggle.

Now, though, she had evidence that she was fully capable of achieving goals that she'd created.

A wonderful way to counter this sense of no/slow progress is to keep a running journal or list of your activities and progress toward your goal. See Part III for some excellent strategies to design this in a way to really support your success.

Mini-exercise

List three instances of what you've been making progress on that you haven't yet given yourself credit for:

1. _____

2. _____

3. _____

You need to get further down the path

It's also possible that while you seem to be making little tangible progress, the "wheels are turning," so to speak, and you're making interior progress. Sometimes there is some internal processing and development that needs to occur before outer advances can be made; something inside needs to gel first.

In these cases, the skill of patiently waiting for clarity as to the most effective and productive way to move forward can be the difference between miserable stuckness and happy triumph.

Kelly had a wonderful idea for a new business project, one that was nicely aligned with her values. She'd been thinking about how to move forward with the vision she had of how it might look, though nothing much seemed to have come of it yet, and it had been months. She'd told others about this idea, and they had been excited for her, and wanted to support her in reaching this vision. Six months later, however, friends and associates were wondering why she had involved herself in other projects and seemed to be making little headway with this more heart-connected effort.

Kelly, too, was beginning to wonder why she wasn't making more of an effort, and was beginning to doubt herself. She couldn't decide if she wasn't managing her time well, or if her priorities were off kilter, or if she was just being plain lazy.

There was, however, another alternative. Perhaps she really was making progress, though it was less tangible than she expected it to be. She had been experimenting mentally with some of her ideas, she'd been making contacts with people who had done similar or related things, and she'd been talking with people who were in her target market about what their needs might be in this area. All of this was percolating and marinating in a positive way, so that when she was ready to take action on it, that action would be informed, inspired, and highly focused. This way, there would be little wasted effort.

Over and over, I find that my clients make greater leaps, untethered by the usual struggle, when they take the time to get clear about their vision, their direction, and their approach, rather than proceeding just so they can feel there is movement toward their goal.

Mini-exercise

What is it you need to have more clarity about before taking appropriate action?

_____

_____

_____

The opportunity isn't yet ripe, even though you don't consciously recognize it

In order for you to be living fully and in accordance with what is right for you, it's necessary to be connected to the inner wisdom that we often ignore. That internal compass is very valuable, and you may have experienced a number of instances when you made poor decisions because you didn't listen to it.

At the very core of procrastination lies the disconnection with the higher wisdom of this interior guidance system.

You may be asking yourself how these are related.

The foundation of a life lived well (and on time!) is being aware of and acting on what is most closely aligned with who you are beyond all the training, the socialization, the conditioning that leads to the shoulds, coulds, and ought-to's. Many, if not most, of us haven't a clue about who we are without being attached to one or more labels that we've come to identify with: doctor or engineer, housewife or parent, non-creative or athlete, assertive or passive. While these may inform the way we spend time or apply ourselves, they are not always accurate, nor do they necessarily hold the keys to satisfaction, validation, respect, or success. What if these are all illusions, the very things keeping us from what we truly want to experience in life?

We've had years, even decades, of "education" that convinces us that we need to be a particular way, have a certain lifestyle, position, career, or play an admired role. Some of us were lucky enough to have personalities, parents, and/or mentors who elicited our truer selves, who created the safe harbor for us to be able to express who we are without being chastised, berated, or punished for it.

Most of us were not so lucky.

We have a choice, though, now that we're adults, to take a closer look at how we spend our energies, what we pursue and how we go after it, what roles and beliefs we've accepted by default or programming. Once we discover what is there, we have a second choice: do we want to re-train ourselves to have new perspectives, goals, and approaches that involve less struggle, effort, time, and discontentment? This will take a bit of re-tooling and some time to fall into place. After all, you've had quite a few years of scripting using the messages you've been operating with.

There is no one path to this reconnection that works for everyone. Some people journal, others meditate. Some play with their children or their pets, or take a solitary walk. Some people pray, while others play. One thing that unites all of these methods is that they involve slowing down and a willingness to not need to be constantly "productive."

Mini-exercise

What will you do to foster patience and prepare yourself internally before taking action?

_____

_____

_____

Busy People

That can be tough on those of us who get some of our "juice" from the label "productive." Who will we be if we are not doing something of use or value? What are we avoiding by being so busy?

We're evading a sense that we're not valuable or worthwhile enough if we don't pull more than our weight. We've bought into the "badge of honor" that if we barely have enough time to go to the bathroom, we must be important and commendable. If we have any spare time it must mean that we're not trying hard enough, that we're somehow slacking off, and the implication is that we won't have the success and respect we so desperately pursue.

I've had clients and friends who simply cringe at the thought of taking a day off, entirely to themselves and without a schedule, to do anything their heart desires in any given moment, even if that means they're headed toward the bookstore to browse, and decide to turn around and go to the park for a stroll. The notion of an entire unscheduled, non-industrious, non-results oriented day, or even an afternoon, is so alien and threatening that they reject even the suggestion of it.

It means that they'll have to simply be, and be with themselves, not doing things for others, not focused on the future, simply enjoying the present. What morals or ideas about proper conduct could be lurking in your view of the world that prevent you from experiencing the present moment fully?

Have there been pleasant events or situations that you could not enjoy because you were always focused on what the next hour, day, or goal was and how you were going to get there?

Don't get me wrong! Goals, planning, strategizing, and doing are good things! That is, until we take them too far.

When clients first develop the skills and start using and practicing the tools of planning, scheduling, and strategizing, they feel that the world is opening up to them. It's no longer such a slog or burden to be productive, efficient, or effective; in fact, it becomes a pleasurable game to see how much one can accomplish, how packed we can make our day.

Within a couple of years, though, these methods become more of a prison. Being so goal, accomplishment, and results focused has started taking its toll. Tiredness, exhaustion, pressure, and stress become more and more draining. Yet, we're very attached to our busy-ness. If we aren't always achieving new, bigger, better successes and triumphs, are we less worthy as people? If we spend some time on ourselves, replenishing our "well" of energy and inspiration, does that make us selfish?

These are certainly the messages and values that most of us have been taught, and they're values I take issue with. I'm not suggesting that we laze around all day and have no goals or intentions.

Biographies of notable and traditionally successful people who have led fulfilling lives are full of evidence that they took the time they needed to restock their personal energy reserves. They made it a priority to ensure that they got the rest and relaxation they needed to perform optimally. This included dropping or delegating what was less important or not the best use of their time.

Our culture has elevated the "do it yourself" attitude to an art. Without questioning it, we've bought into the notion that in order to be successful we can't have anyone else's help. If it's not done all by our lonesome, it's not a true success, and we're not really deserving. By default (women, in the 21st century, especially) we think that if we're not handling it all, there must be something less than wonderful about us. Thankfully, there are those people who have railed and rebelled, and had great triumphs without needing to "do it all." They set an encouraging example for the rest of us.

Mini-exercise

How do you, or do you plan to, replenish your well of
energy and inspiration on a regular basis?

_____

_____

_____

The window of opportunity has closed

During one of my "Anticrastinate Your Way to
Success" presentations for Sony Electronics, one
particular woman kept on referring to a housewarming
party she had been putting off. After she had mentioned
this a number of times, I asked her when she had moved
into her house. We all waited breathlessly for her answer,
which came haltingly, "Five years ago."

It was time for her to move on! The house had to be
pretty warm after five years, and if it wasn't, a party
wasn't going to help. Who amongst her friends and
colleagues (whom she had been promising for years she'd
have over for this party) would really believe they were
actually coming to a housewarming party? It would be
more like a party that was apologizing for not having a
housewarming party.

You're probably wondering why she hadn't had the
party (or perhaps you're not!). There were details that

hadn't yet been completed that she felt must be done before she could have people over. Window treatments needed to be put up, a new kitchen floor installed, and there were still a couple of boxes that hadn't been unpacked from the move, etc. She wanted the house to be perfect before she could schedule her party. Does any of this sound familiar?

What a relief it was for her to be able to let go of this belief that she still had to schedule a housewarming party. At this point, nobody was expecting her to have a party, and it was time for her to give herself permission to let the idea go.

"Historical" goals, those which you've had for quite some time (perhaps for twenty years!) and have never realized, can fit into this category. You may have tried various methods, self-help books, therapy, but nothing has worked, or worked for the long term. While it may be that these are simply poorly designed objectives, or "shoulds," it may also be that they are no longer relevant, even though you've been hanging on to them.

Do you have long-term aspirations you've been pursuing for years, with either little progress or little staying power? It may be time to re-evaluate them. Here are a few things to consider:

- Are they still pertinent to your life and lifestyle?
- Although they might once have been realistic, is that still the case?
- Does this goal *really* still matter to you?

- Are you honestly willing to make the changes that would be required to achieve this end?

If you answered yes to any or all of these, please refer to the Part III of this book. If you answered no to one or more, it may be time to dump the goal.

Mini-exercise

What aspiration that has not come true might it be time to put aside, at least for now?

_____

_____

_____

Chapter 5
The Importance of What's Important

"Time is nature's way of making sure that everything doesn't happen at once."
—Source Unknown

There are other, more important priorities.

Amongst the entire range of productive procrastination, this category will by far be the one with the largest number of goals in it.

While some of the things that are on your procrastination list will definitely need to get done, it's possible that some, compared to the most important, timely, and necessary of them, you'd be quite wise to put off. As we continue to stretch our abilities and evolve as a species (ever-faster, higher, longer, stronger sports records and other record accomplishments are evidence of this), we expect more and more of ourselves. We push ourselves beyond what we believe to be our limits, and it's now become expected that our level of achievements will always be on the upswing. It's a double-edge sword.

Life has become more complex, and there are so many things to keep up with. In the past twenty years, we've been forced to make more choices about many things, and to be educated about those choices. Telephone communication is one of them. It used to be that Ma Bell had a monopoly on telephone service. There was one company (and 70 or so years ago, for most Americans, there wasn't even that!) and no choice. Even after the Bell breakup, there wasn't much choice, but it wasn't long until we had to choose who we would use for long distance service vs. regional service. More recently, with the advent of cell phones, if we want to jump on that bandwagon, we have to choose a provider, a telephone, a plan, additional account options, as well as whether we get wired long distance through our cable provider (if we have one, and that's another new option/decision, along with internet service), ad nauseum.

Simply put, there's just so much more stuff to keep up with. Unless you've made a very conscious decision to live a very simple life, you're finding yourself running a little harder every year to keep up.

"We all live in a 31 flavors world. The more complex the world, the bigger the challenges we have. One hundred years ago, we lived in a chocolate and vanilla world; our choices were limited, and the directions we could take were limited. Now, we have so many choices. In some ways, it's easier to be successful, but it's also easier to fail...it's easy to make wrong choices. All of those choices become overwhelming. Success today is more complex; there are more opportunities for both

success and failure. It's odd, but it's the truth."

Ivan Misner, Founder & CEO of Business
Networking International

The more complex life gets, the more crucial it has become to be selective and discriminating about how we spend our time and energy. Because it's more and more tempting to be diverted by the many possibilities available to us (many times more than there were just fifty or sixty years ago), the need to get focused on what will serve us in the long run is more important than ever. At the same time, it's getting harder and harder to determine which of the many options at our disposal are the more important ones.

As a result, what happens is that each moment we're doing one thing, we're plagued by the sense that we should be doing something else, no matter what it is we're applying ourselves to. Do you recognize yourself in the following examples? While returning phone calls, you think you should be completing that report that's due soon. When you're reading the newspaper because you want to be informed about what's happening in the world, it seems that perhaps instead you should be taking care of some details that have been lingering; when you're spending time with your family, you're also aware that work issues need to be addressed and are nagging at you. You're not really present for much of anything, and rarely feel that you're doing the right thing at any given time.

The accompanying overwhelm and stress this produces drains your energy and significantly reduces your capacity to be productive and effective. If it helps, know that many people are in exactly the same boat as you. And you don't have to sink!

Taking the time to plan and get organized, while it seems like a good idea, feels uncomfortable. Taking even *more* time out of your busy day to plan it when you could be doing something productive would be nice, if only you had more time! Perhaps you've tried this, but then got off track for some reason or so busy that you gave it up or forgot about it.

I haven't done formal research with my clients, but anecdotal evidence suggests that spending ten to fifteen minutes once per week creating a plan for the week, and ten to twenty minutes in daily planning and checking against that plan results in a 25-50% increase in achieving the goals we set for ourselves, along with a much greater sense of control and accomplishment. Fewer details slip through the cracks.

It's certainly worthwhile to question how we spend our time and our money. While financial habits are not the subject of this book, when examining why we procrastinate it's wise to evaluate how your spend your time currently, as well as how you'd like that to change for the better. There are many ways of doing this; an effective way you may not have tried is by using the Where Has The Time Gone Worksheet included here. You might also want to experiment with the "Prioritizing Your To-Do List" form that follows it.

Worksheet

Where has the time gone?

There are three worksheets in this exercise:

- the sample below for illustrative purposes
- a blank for evaluating how you're currently using your time and energy
- another blank for redesigning how you *want* to spend your daily/weekly/monthly life.

These estimates are fairly conservative, but general; your tasks and times allotted may vary considerably. You may work more or fewer hours (time allotment includes commute—see footnotes), not have kids (or pets) at home to care for, nor do your own cleaning or errands. However, you may spend more time eating out, participating in volunteer activities, engaging in your hobby, attending social events, watching TV, exercising, or talking on the telephone, for example. Additionally, this list is also not comprehensive—there will be other activities you engage in regularly that aren't listed. You may want more leisure or personal time than is shown below.

To make it easier to compute, we're using a weekly value. If you figure that you spend about 4 hours per month on something, it would equal about an hour per week. If you watch television for 3 hours a day most days of the week, that would equal around 21 hours per week. If you go to the gym 3 times a week for an hour each time, you'd add three hours plus your travel time to and from the gym. You get the idea.

There are 168 hours in a week. Allowing 7 hours daily for sleep and 1.5 hours daily for showering, dressing, and eating all meals, the weekly available time is reduced down to 108.5 hours.

I've classified the tasks as follows, so that you'll have a more realistic idea of what areas you might want to cut back on, and which you'd like to increase:

o=obligation/responsibility
p=personal
l=leisure
w=work

Sample Template

Activity	Type	Hour Per Day/month	Hours Per Week
Work #	w		50.00
Child care * (or elder care)	o & p	2 hours/day	14.00
Kids Activities ^	o	1 hour/day	7.00
E-mail/Internet/voicemail	p	1hour/day	7.00
Hobby	l		3.00
Phone calls	p	1hour/day	7.00
Pet care	o	½ hour/day	3.50
Cleaning house/laundry	o		4.00
Errands %	o	1 hour/day	7.00
Exercise	p	45 min/day	3.75
Volunteer position	o	3 hours/mo	3.00
Garden/lawn care	o & l		1.00
Personal/home admin~	p		2.00
Personal care+	p	½ hour/day	3.50
Reading for work	w	1 hour/day	7.00
Reading newspaper	p	½ hour/day	3.50
Reading (leisure)	l	½ hour/day	3.50
Watching TV/movies	l	1 hour/day	7.00
Socializing/friends	l		3.00
Quality time w spouse	l		3.00
Total			**140.00**

o=obligation/responsibility
p=personal
l=leisure
w=work

\# : includes commute

* : prep for school, prepping meals and cleanup, help with homework, putting to bed, quality time, etc.

^ : athletic, scholastic, social activities, including transportation

% : includes bank, post office, shopping, dry cleaner, buying gifts, etc.

~ : paying bills, having work done at house, tidying up, fixing things, staying organized, dealing with details, etc.

+ : manicure/pedicure, getting haircut, doctor's appointments, etc.

The listed tasks with their estimates added up to 140 hours per week! You'd have to give up over 30 hours of sleep to get all this done! Now it's your turn. Use the template below to evaluate how you're currently spending your time, and then how you'd *like* to spend your time.

How I'm Currently Using My Time and Energy

Use the template below to evaluate how you're currently spending your time.

Activity	Type	Hour Per Day/month	Hours Per Week
Work #			
Child care * (or elder care)			
Kids Activities ^			
E-mail/Internet/voicemail			
Hobby			
Phone calls			
Pet care			
Cleaning house/laundry			
Errands $^{\%}$			
Exercise			
Volunteer position			
Garden/lawn care			
Personal/home admin$^{\sim}$			
Personal care^{+}			
Reading for work			
Reading newspaper			
Reading (leisure)			
Watching TV/movies			
Socializing/friends			
Quality time w spouse			
Total			

o=obligation/responsibility
p=personal
l=leisure
w=work

\# : includes commute

* : prep for school, prepping meals and cleanup, help with homework, putting to bed, quality time, etc.

^ : athletic, scholastic, social activities, including transportation

% : includes bank, post office, shopping, dry cleaner, buying gifts, etc.

~ : paying bills, having work done at house, tidying up, fixing things, staying organized, dealing with details, etc.

\+ : manicure/pedicure, getting haircut, doctor's appointments, etc.

The Importance of What's Important

Comments:

_____

_____

_____

_____

_____

_____

_____

_____

_____

_____

_____

_____

_____

_____

How I'd Like to Redesign Use of My Time & Energy

Use the template below to create a new plan to describe how you'd *like* to spend your time.

Activity	Type	Hour Per Day/month	Hours Per Week
Work #			
Child care * (or elder care)			
Kids Activities ^			
E-mail/Internet/voicemail			
Hobby			
Phone calls			
Pet care			
Cleaning house/laundry			
Errands %			
Exercise			
Volunteer position			
Garden/lawn care			
Personal/home admin~			
Personal care+			
Reading for work			
Reading newspaper			
Reading (leisure)			
Watching TV/movies			
Socializing/friends			
Quality time w spouse			
Total			

o=obligation/responsibility
p=personal
l=leisure
w=work

: includes commute

* : prep for school, prepping meals and cleanup, help with homework, putting to bed, quality time, etc.

^ : athletic, scholastic, social activities, including transportation

% : includes bank, post office, shopping, dry cleaner, buying gifts, etc.

~ : paying bills, having work done at house, tidying up, fixing things, staying organized, dealing with details, etc.

+ : manicure/pedicure, getting haircut, doctor's appointments, etc.

Comments:

_____

_____

_____

_____

_____

_____

_____

_____

_____

_____

_____

_____

_____

The Importance of What's Important

"Time has a wonderful way of weeding out the trivial."

—Richard Ben Sapir

So...what did you get out of that exercise? Did it give you a whack upside the head about the way you're expending your life energy every day? Were you surprised at how it added up, and what areas you hadn't realized you were devoting much more time to than you'd like?

Even if you have a current attachment to getting everything done, it's more effective and appropriate to remove some goals from your primary list (that is, if you keep a list) to a secondary one. If you have difficulty in determining what is the priority, try using the "Prioritizing Your To-Do List" worksheet below. This is strongly recommended, especially if you're the type of person for whom everything seems important. Obviously, some things are more important than others, so spending time on them is a higher priority.

I'll guess that you'd have to be a super-hero with special powers in order to accomplish everything you've listed. That's alright. Actually, that's the point. No, I'm not selling special powers, or even suggesting that you consider how you might pursue super-hero status. Instead, I've got some other ideas.

Say No

If it's not already on your plate, prevent more

overload by heading things off at the pass. This means politely and diplomatically turning down requests for volunteering, obligations, doing certain favors, and some activities you might be considering. You'll also be served by limiting your kids' activities so you don't feel like a constant chauffeur and by limiting or eliminating certain chores that aren't necessary but you think you "should" start doing. Keep a tight rein on the amount of time you spend on activities like reading/writing e-mail, internet surfing, and watching the new reality TV shows, mediocre sitcoms, and heavily advertised talk shows (yes, you can tell I have a bias!).

One of the challenges of Saying No is that it requires you develop some boundaries for yourself and language that feels comfortable. Just saying "No" isn't something that comes easily for many of us, especially those who have bought into the idea that we should sacrifice and make every effort to help others. While this isn't to suggest that you should be insensitive to the needs of others, you'll be less available to others if you don't pay attention to your own needs first.

It's likely you think turning people down will seem selfish, inconsiderate, and uncaring. Think of the times when you asked something of someone else, and they declined. Did you go into judgment about them, or did you simply accept that they weren't available at that time?

Saying no will take some practice, and it will help if you have some responses that you're at ease with. Here are some possibilities.

When someone is asking for your volunteer help or a favor, responses such as:

- "Thanks so much for your vote of confidence! To take that on, I'd want to do a thorough job for you, but unfortunately, my plate is really full right now."
- "I can't do it at this time, but perhaps in the future." (if you really mean that)
- "I'm not available for new activities at the moment."
- "I've got another appointment at that time and won't be able to help you."

Be careful not to make statements that aren't true or that you don't really feel, such as that you'd love to do something (when you really wouldn't love to), or that they should call you next time they need something (but you'd prefer them not to).

You may have used the following strategy with your kids, but delaying a decision can be a great tactic to use with anyone making a request of you.

- "Let me think about it."
- "I'll let you know tomorrow"
- "Give me a few days to consider it."
- "I'm not sure right now."

This is especially effective because that person might find someone else in the interim, or may no longer have the need at that later time. Certainly, if you've committed to letting someone know in the future, follow through and let them know of your decision.

You needn't explain yourself. In fact, the more you try to give reasons, the bigger the hole you dig for yourself, and the less good both you and the other person feel about the whole thing.

As you get more practice in saying no, it becomes easier. You'll develop your own style and way of responding. Eventually, you may easily be able to simply say, "No, thank you!" in a kindly but firm way.

What if what you're Saying No to are your own activities and indulgences? It helps to take a look at the activity or indulgence and determine what the cost of doing that thing is; what will it prevent you from having time for? What is the cost of not having enough time for the other things you'd have to limit or give up?

Everyone has a need to treat themselves sometimes; everyone's needs differ as far as frequency and intensity of luxury, indulgence, or simple relaxation. Just because someone you know or admire has a particular attitude toward slowing down, or stopping to smell the roses doesn't mean that their needs and tastes will match yours. Of course, this isn't an excuse for going into full time or permanent relaxation mode! However, if there are a couple of television programs you absolutely love, allow them to be a treasured part of your life, but stop watching indiscriminately. Surf the net, but keep the time you spend on it in line with the bigger picture of what you want in your life.

Mini-exercise

List three things you're considering incorporating into your life that you've decided to Say No to:

1. _____

2. _____

3. _____

Let Go

What is in your life already that can you give up entirely?

Especially recommended for jettisoning are some ideas of who we "should" be, and chores, possessions, and/or positions we hold that no longer serve who we want to be. It also means not watching television mindlessly, for example, or answering telephone calls that come in the middle of other activities (or at times when it would be better to let the message go into voicemail). We can't leave out letting go of perfectionism. We've covered that in more depth in Chapter 3, in case you missed it.

Included in letting go might be volunteer positions you've taken on that no longer fit you or align with how you want to spend your precious time. Perhaps you've come to partly identify with or pin some of your self-worth on your volunteer activities (yes, I've done that!). Because you give up a particular position in one organization doesn't mean you can't take on another one there or somewhere new and more fitting for your values, now or at some point later when your schedule might be more flexible. By letting go of the position, it does not mean that you no longer value the mission of the organization or initiative, or that you are selfish. If you're procrastinating on your volunteer duties and not meeting deadlines, it's especially important that you free up the position so someone else can step in and do them.

Which brings up the next point about volunteering (or doing particular favors regularly for people): you're concerned that nobody else will do it. This is certainly a valid concern, but ask yourself: are *you* getting it done?

If the answer is yes, first of all celebrate your timely completion of those tasks! It may seem like it will take more work to find someone to fill your shoes than to simply do the work yourself. There are many ways to find a replacement for yourself. If you find that you're really reluctant to take action to find someone else, what might be happening is that you are hanging on to the power, influence, status, or respect you get from others for carrying out your duties, even if those rewards of the position are slim. Ask yourself whether the energy and time the position is costing you is worth the rewards of the position, and whether there might be a more satisfying way of contributing in the future.

If you're not getting the work of your volunteer position done, you're not serving the effort or organization well and you might even be hindering them. It's always best to resign from the position so someone else can take it over and do it justice; both you and the other people involved will feel relieved. Even though you made some kind of commitment when you accepted the position or role, it doesn't mean that by resigning you're admitting you're a bad person for not following through with it. It means you're an honorable person who wants to make sure the job gets done, even though you had good intentions and it simply hasn't worked out. If you care about what the group thinks of you, they will feel better about you the sooner you recognize and communicate that you aren't going to be able to fulfill the role rather than dragging things out.

What are other regular roles you play or responsibilities you're in charge of that you might let go of? Are you doing (or putting off!) chores that have gotten overly complicated, certain phone calls to friends or relatives that might be shortened or made less frequently, or might you want to cut your losses on certain financial drains that are costing you money, effectiveness, and self-esteem?

Craft projects you've started and haven't completed, hobbies you've taken up and haven't been keeping up with (are you still even really interested?), the idea that you can do all your re-organizing and de-cluttering, creating a full financial plan and/or doing home repairs by yourself, are other candidates of letting go of (or delegating).

Other aspects of your life that may play a role in being overwhelmed and result in procrastination (that you might want to let go of) are needing to open junk mail and e-mail, magazine, newspaper, and e-mail subscriptions, clutter, needing to read many career-related industry publications,

Then, of course, there are the less productive habits

to reduce or let go of completely. Too much television, e-mail, shopping, computer games, internet surfing, instant messaging, etc. cut into your productive time substantially. You know what those activities are. You don't necessary need to cut them out entirely, and as a matter of fact some of them, in moderation can be used as rewards for completing small chunks of what you've been procrastinating about. Then again, if you've found that one or more of those activities is somewhat "addictive" for you, it will probably be more effective, for the moment, at least, to refrain from doing those things at all.

List three things you're doing now that you're going to Let Go of:

1. _____

2. _____

3. _____

Delegate

Maybe you shouldn't be doing it yourself!

Wherever and with whatever you can, to whomever will do a decent enough job, do not focus on perfection and get some help. If it's affordable, hire someone to clean (it took me decades to bring myself to do this, by the way, but it's very worth it!), mow your lawn, paint the house, help you organize your closets, files, attic, or basement, or prepare your tax return. (Too bad we can't delegate flossing our teeth or exercising, eh?) Ask family members and friends to help. Arrange a barter; get a neighbor or a neighbor's kid to do it for you.

Be creative and open to possibilities. This is one area in which I usually hear significant pushback from clients and teleclass participants. They say, "That won't work because..." or "Yeah, but...," or "I can't afford that." With some tasks, it's possible that you can't afford *not* to. If you're reluctant to allow someone to help you, or to have them see your mess or less-than-perfect-ness, it's definitely going to be a limiting factor in overcoming your procrastination inclination. Don't look for how it *won't* work, look for how it *could*.

List three things you're doing now that you will Delegate to others:

1. _____

2. _____

3. _____

Prioritizing

Now that you've been whittling down the items on your to-do list, it's a good time to take a look at what's left. It's very possible that you haven't completed, or even attempted, a number of tasks simply because there have been bigger, more important priorities that needed to be handled first.

It's inevitable that while many tasks seem like they are priorities in the moment, from a more elevated perspective they are of less consequence. One of the best ways to reduce overwhelm is to reduce your load. While it may need to get done, it may not need to get done *right now*.

It might be a good time to compare each task or project against the others that are left on your list to get a good idea of what is less of a priority, and what is most necessary and immediate. Through this process you may even be able to cross off additional list entries. Below is an exercise designed to help you determine what needs more immediate attention, and what is appropriate to put off for this moment.

If you find, through this exercise, that you've appropriately been putting off certain things that are lower on the priority scale, congratulate yourself for following your internal wisdom. By the way, this doesn't mean you should put them off forever, necessarily. Part II of this book will help you discover whether this procrastination is productive or destructive. Once you have that information, you'll know whether you need Part III to complete the task before it could turn into an even bigger problem.

Prioritizing Your To-Do List

It's crucial that we learn to distinguish "important" from "urgent." In The Seven Habits of Highly Effective People, *Stephen R. Covey suggests, "Importance...has to do with results. If something is important, it contributes to your mission, your values, and your high priority goals. Urgent matters are usually visible. They press on us; they insist on action. They're often popular with others. They're usually right in front of us. And often they are pleasant, easy, or fun to do. But so often they are unimportant!"*

Assign a number from 10 (highest) to 1 (lowest) to each item, first by importance, and then by urgency. Something is a 10 only if it is necessary, has significant consequences if it's not taken care of, and, in the overall scheme of your life, is something you'd truly and deeply regret not doing. There aren't many things in life that rate a 10. If, for instance, the steel belts on your tires are starting to show, putting off getting new tires could have some very serious and damaging consequences, and you might truly regret not taking care of it, perhaps rating an 8 or a 9. On the other hand, if you use your car only for occasional short trips to the grocery store, replacing your tires may be of somewhat lesser urgency and importance, especially as compared to some other tasks, and you might assign only a 3 or 4 to this task.

Be aware that your tendency might be to rate everything as an 8, 9, or 10 but resist the urge. Remember that you're scoring each one on their own merits, but also scoring each against all the others

Total the two numbers you assign to each. It may turn out that one or more score low relative to the others. If that's the case, you can feel more comfortable putting them off to tomorrow or next week and put your efforts today into those tasks that have the highest totals. Once you've completed this, schedule each item for a particular date and time in your date book or calendar. You'll be much more likely to do them when they're scheduled because you've made more of a commitment to doing them.

Item	Importance	Urgency	Total
1.			
2.			
3.			
4.			
5.			
6.			
7.			
8.			
9.			
10.			
11.			
12.			

Chapter 6
Ready, Set, Wait

By now you're probably feeling a sense of relief. It lightens your load a lot when so many things you thought you should have done days, weeks, even years ago would have been a poor use of your time and efforts. Pretty liberating, isn't it?

This chapter discusses another form of productive procrastination—you're not destructively procrastinating if there is insufficient information to make a good decision or take appropriate action.

It is actually productive to procrastinate when you don't have all of the necessary information. If you've ever made decisions or taken action before you were fully informed, and you regretted it, you get my drift. Sometimes taking action prematurely is just inconvenient, other times it's really embarrassing, and occasionally it's completely disastrous. Those of you who have bought boats, horses, pets, or even houses without understanding how much time, effort, expense, and frustration could be involved, or those of you who felt some kind of pressure to get married, and wedded someone before you knew enough about them to ensure marital bliss (or at least a stable relationship), are probably nodding your heads in agreement.

Sometimes the best course of action is simply to wait until you have more data. Your mental chatter, as well as family and friends, may be chastising you for not taking action, but if you are about to take a next step and recognize that there are factors you haven't taken into consideration, or knowledge you need, or conclusions you haven't come to, it's a mistake to move forward just for action's sake. You've been there, done that, and don't want to do it again.

Before you take action, remember that you need clarity, not speed, in making wise decisions.

Before I go any farther describing this type of productive procrastination, it's worth adding a caveat: if you're something of a perfectionist, or someone who is uncomfortable with risk, with a tendency to put things off indefinitely, justifying the delay by saying you're looking for more and more information, this may not be productive procrastination. See Part II of this book to learn more about how to tell the difference between productive, neutral, and destructive procrastination.

What you don't know can stop you in your tracks

This form of productive procrastination became clear to me one day long ago as I was leading teleconference classes on getting organized. A participant in the class was belittling herself because she had been meaning to get organized for a long time, and had even scheduled it into her calendar, but she still hadn't done it. I asked her to imagine getting started with the project immediately after she got off the phone from the teleconference, and as she did, it turned out that she hadn't a clue how the organizing process works. She didn't know where to start, what to do first, or second or third, for that matter. Until that moment she believed she was just putting the project off instead of understanding she needed more information before she could begin.

Similarly, one of my early clients, Katie, had never learned time or space management skills. She saw herself as disadvantaged and behind the eight ball because of it, but like most of us, she'd never had good examples nor was she offered a class in school about how to maximize time and keep stuff organized. And like most of us, she expected she should just know how. Katie and I worked together over a period of a few months, bringing her up to speed on those skills. As she made progress in applying the new techniques she was learning, her talent-coach business, which had been languishing, took off.

If you're a manager or executive, and your employees are procrastinating on particular projects, it could be that they don't know how to approach or execute those projects, and they're afraid to ask, for fear they'll look bad. See Part IV for solutions to this challenge.

Mini-exercise

Scan your to-do list, and see if there are any items on there that could fall into this category.

When pondering is better than action

Sometimes there's an internal decision you need to make, one that's vital to the project or task, before you can take a next step.

After selling his business a couple of years before, Lucas had been working as a consultant to the company that bought it from him. We'll call that company Allied Products. While being called in to handle crises appealed to his ego, working with Allied's executive team over the last two years as they mishandled the business into a limping, struggling mess was draining and disagreeable to him. They were paying him well, though. The money was pretty good but, honestly, he said, he didn't really need the money.

It was clear to me, as Lucas and I discussed options, that he really wanted out, but when we'd look at that option, conflicting desires surfaced, as they always do when action doesn't follow intention. You see, Lucas felt something of an obligation to help the people who worked for the company. As we explored the idea of leaving further, he admitted to himself that whether he stayed or left, he'd be doing the equivalent of rearranging deck chairs on the Titanic. Allied Product's top executives were sorely lacking in leadership skills, and the company would probably go under within half a year. Nothing Lucas could do would really change that, except perhaps make that lingering, torturous collapse longer and more drawn out.

As we continued to examine options, I realized there was a missing piece: what would Lucas do, how would he spend his time, if he left his consultancy with Allied? Since he had a strong work ethic, and he enjoyed turning businesses around, he wasn't about to just retire, plus he had some financial obligations he was carrying. The biggest reason Lucas was waffling was because he had not yet really thought about or explored opportunities for the future.

Once he gave himself permission to look more closely at what he might want to do, and had some discussions with potential partners in a promising venture, ending the consultancy was more and more appealing. Lucas's vital internal question was, "What will I do with myself and how will I ensure my financial security if I leave?" Until he had some answers to that question, taking action would be premature. Sometimes you're just missing a strategy and plan of action.

Someone Else's Information

Might you be waiting for information or answers from others to move forward? Stuart, an accountant, was unhappy with himself for putting off working on his clients' tax returns, having to cram so much work in so close to the tax deadline. It turned out his self-judgment was unwarranted though, because as we drilled down deeper and I asked for information about specific clients, it suddenly dawned on him that he *couldn't* work on their returns because they hadn't gotten all their financial data to him yet. As we continued to discuss individual clients, again and again this same theme repeated.

One of my goals for this year was to reduce the environmental impact of my lifestyle and home. In July I attended a local Renewable Energy Expo, and found some vendors for solar photovoltaic systems. Installing one of these systems would use a clean renewable resource—the sun—and dramatically reduce our home's need for power from the regional utility, power that would be adding to global warming. By September, each time I'd look at my goal, I'd ask myself why I hadn't completed it (assuming I was procrastinating) until I remembered that the vendor I'd chosen still hadn't gotten back to me with an estimate. It took about eight or nine calls until I finally had the information I needed to make a decision or put down a deposit. Like many of us, I found myself "going there," doubting my ability to get this done within my (self-imposed) deadline.

When coaching managers in businesses, I frequently find that at least some of the assignments they're dragging their feet on are not due to their own lack of action, but because a colleague, co-worker, or employee hasn't given them a necessary report, despite requesting it from that person.

Mini-exercise

Who are you waiting for information from before you can take more action on something:

_____

_____

_____

Needing to make the "right" choice.

You might not realize it, but you may not be taking action because you're concerned that you have to make "the one right choice." It's a fallacy to believe in the "right" choice mentality, and it's an illusion, too, since a "right" choice for you may be a wrong choice by someone else's standards. All choices involve risk, there's just no getting around it. Some choices involve a lot more risk than others.

Added to that, we feel that once we've made a choice it's written in stone, and we have to stick with it through thick and thin. What a limiting perspective! There really aren't very many decisions we make in life that we can't later adjust. While it may feel "right" at the moment, it may be a wrong choice by next month, next year, or next decade, as we've grown, learned, met new people, are offered, or create, new opportunities.

There's certainly been cultural pressure to not change your mind about something, no matter the cost. If you identify with this "right" choice inclination, you got this message from your parents, teachers, religious leaders, and other authority figures. Fortunately, the pressure to comply with this notion has been changing. Worldwide, there's evidence that people are more understanding about and accepting of needing to be flexible and allow for correction and tweaking where desirable.

What would your decision be, and what action would you take, if you knew that you could change your mind if things didn't work out the way you'd hoped? What would Plan B and Plan C look like?

Usually our expectations get in our way. When you expect that your results will look a particular way, you're blind to how the way things turn out might be even better, might serve your interests even more perfectly than you'd planned for, even though they look different. Sometimes we can't see how right a different result is until much later. I've learned, through my own journey and through witnessing those of my clients, that there's always some gift hidden in how things turn out, even it if looks pretty bad in the moment.

Mini-exercise:

What decisions that require "right" choices are you delaying making?

_____

_____

_____

The Eleventh Hour

Are you someone who categorizes themselves as an "eleventh hour" person, someone who waits until the very last minute to complete the task or project?

For most of us, the eleventh hour is characterized by dread, deep anxiety, crabbiness, and an inability to focus well because of worry that we'll overshoot the deadline. For hours, days, weeks, or even months, the stress builds, so incrementally we don't even notice it. We may or may not realize how it affects the other things we're doing, and even our general sense of self-control and competence. While we know we'll eventually get to it, in the meanwhile it decreases the focus and energy we have available for all the other things we must get done.

The result of this last-minute labor is often poor due to insufficient research, errors that we haven't had time to catch, hastily reached conclusions, and inadequate thought about the quality of the finished outcome. And that's if we don't miss our deadline! Does this sound familiar? Yes, eleventh hour cramming can be the bad kind of procrastination.

Understanding how you operate, though, might allow you to be an effective eleventh hour person. You can train yourself to do this well. Would you like your effort to result in superb, first-class work? I'll bet you would! Is it possible to use the pressure to focus your energy and provide the adrenalin and intensity to do an exemplary job? It most definitely is. I wouldn't suggest doing this all day, every day, though, as it leads to burnout quickly.

Perhaps you're already a natural eleventh hour person, someone who does get the job done on time and well. You thrive on the pressure of the deadline, and the focus it requires. The closer it gets to the cut-off date (or hour), the more psyched you become. You know what you need to have in place and you've got it; you know what you need to do and you do it. While you haven't been at least seemingly working on it, in the back of your mind you've been working out some of the ideas, format, direction, or flow of what you'll be completing later. And you do almost all the "work" at the last minute. Even though you feel you've done a good job and are happy with the end result (and so are the people who pay you!), there's still a nagging internal voice berating you for waiting so long and rushing to complete things at the last possible moment ("It could have been better." But how much better, really?). Here's my suggestion: accept and embrace rather than resist this tendency. You've got a good thing going!

If you know you perform best under a deadline, give up the nagging negative self-talk about doing things at the last minute. If it really works well for you, go with it! It's a splendid form of productive procrastination. Spend the "first ten hours" giving attention to whatever else is important, and let go of the pinching, energy-draining internal voicemail that says you're a loser for waiting until the last minute.

Could it be that while you're doing some of the internal or more informal research or background preparation, you're just not working on the final stage of the project? For instance, you're doing some internet research, speaking with friends or colleagues, have asked for some information and are waiting for it, or are sorting through possible next steps, but haven't actually made the decision or acted on it or written the report, etc. You only recognize completion, or the last stage before completion, as a measure of progress. Meanwhile, progress *is* happening anyway, but you're not able to appreciate it.

Sadly, most of us are just not effective 11th hour persons. They are a rare few. The rest of us, though, can coach ourselves into using the eleventh hour concept more satisfactorily. It could be that you aren't skilled at estimating how long things take you to accomplish, or you habitually underestimate the amount of time it takes to get something done. It's possible that you don't take into account some inevitable interruptions or other responsibilities that might get in the way. We'll look at how to do this in Part III.

Part II:

Procrastination Identification

Chapter 7
When Procrastination Affects You

Now that it's clear that some of what you've been labeling as procrastination really might not be what you usually think of as procrastination (i.e. bad), how do you know whether it's productive, destructive, or even neutral?

Before I share with you some rule-of-thumb indicators that will help you determine whether action is truly needed, or if you can (and should) continue putting something off, at least for the moment, I need to give you a broader perspective since, ultimately, that's what distinguishes smart from…not-so-smart.

There's also "neutral" procrastination—neither a particularly desirable way to reallocate your time and energy, nor procrastination that has enough negative impact to focus on. If it's neutral, put it aside and revisit in a few weeks.

When distinguishing the productive from destructive forms, I'd love to be able to just tell you to ask yourself, "are the consequences of procrastinating with this particular activity really, truly to my detriment, and I am unwilling to pay that price?" While it's a good overview qualifier, I've found over and over that a more detailed explanation is necessary before you can answer that question effectively.

When clients or workshop participants tell me that not balancing their checkbook (or joining a gym, or getting their tax receipts in order for the accountant) is destructive procrastination, I ask them how not taking action is harming them. They respond that it makes them feel badly about themselves. Okay, but it doesn't mean that inaction on those things, as stand-alone facts, qualifies as destructive. Unless there's a tangible ramification that you'll forfeit something you already have, it doesn't count as destructive. It may be neutral, sometimes even positive.

If you're not balancing your checkbook and because of that you're bouncing checks, paying late fees, and destroying your credit, okay, *that's* destructive! But if there is no consequence greater than not knowing exactly how much is in your account because you're applying yourself to other areas that are higher priority, that's neutral. Understand, I'm not suggesting or recommending that anyone neglect balancing their checkbook, nor am I giving them an excuse to do so! But there are other options, like delegating the activity to another family member, a bookkeeper, an accountant, or trustworthy friend. Rather than reaching back months or years to start your reconciling from the time you got off track, you can start fresh as of today.

Lindy believes she is destructively procrastinating by not making cold calls to prospective buyers. She thinks this is the case because she doesn't have the money she'd have if she made more sales. But she isn't losing what she already has; she is only forfeiting a possibility. She can pay her bills this month, even though it would be a lot more comfortable to have additional income. In my book, that's not destructive procrastination—nothing is really lost—Lindy isn't suffering in any way except that she's heaping the self-blame on. Besides, cold calling may not be a very effective means for Lindy to reach her goal. She tells me she hates cold calling, dreads it. It turns out that she doesn't even think it's going to have good results, but the people in her office think making cold calls is the thing to do to make more sales. Instead, as we're discussing it, I ask Lindy to access her wisdom about this, and to refer to her experience. There's a change in the tone of her voice as she tells me she loves going out to eat with prospects, and enjoys the relationships that develop that way. Within a few weeks, Lindy is acting on this wisdom and her sales are increasing. Hmmm. Was not making cold calls really destructive procrastination? Not so much. Actually, it comes close to being productive.

In this chapter, we'll focus on when procrastination seems to affect you alone. Recognize, though, that we don't live in a vacuum. Unless you're single, with no family, friends, pets, co-workers, bosses, or clients, your procrastinating ways are likely to affect *someone else* in some way. Your health and your financial situation will affect your ability and availability. You might not be able to take a hike along a beautiful trail with friends, or live to see your daughter's wedding. You might not be able to afford to go out to dinner with your buddies, or go on vacation with friends who want your company, so you may get left out...or feel left out.

Even so, some things are still more personal in nature. How do you know whether some perceived personal procrastination is productive—or not?

How necessary is it?

Some things are more necessary than others. Filing income tax returns is necessary if you don't want to get in trouble with the government, for instance. If keeping your teeth is a priority for you, brushing and flossing them is necessary. It's necessary to decrease your spending and/or increase your income, make informed buying decisions, and apply money toward your debts if you want to be debt-free (not to mention financially independent). The necessary test hinges on what you want for yourself, whether you are truly committed to getting it, and whether you're willing to abide by the consequences of not doing it. If you don't care about the interest, late charges, possible legal and accounting fees for not filing your tax returns, if you're looking forward to wearing dentures, or if you plan to never retire and always have debt, then taking action on those things mentioned above isn't necessary.

It does take a bit of experimentation to know where the line between necessary and desired is. While your dentist will advise you to floss after every meal (desired, at least for some people), once per day, or four times per week, may be enough to result in healthy teeth and gums.

You can pay down your debt more rapidly by radically reducing your expenditures, but where will the balance be between what seems sustainable and what seems too draconian? It's different for everyone. Would you rather be done with your debt quickly? If so, what level or degree of delayed gratification are you willing to set for yourself?

You may decide that it's not worth it to you to do much toward these things. I'm not kidding. Many people do. Often, they don't recognize they have a choice, or that they're making a choice not to take action. They kid themselves into believing they'll get around to it eventually. Unaware, they abdicate responsibility for themselves and their lives.

If you know what to do and you know how to do it, but just aren't doing it, it's procrastination. Whether it's necessary or not is based on your values, and determines whether it's productive or destructive procrastination. While you certainly would prefer to not pay taxes late (or pay them at all!), to have large dental bills or lose your teeth, or be in debt, are you *really* prepared to do *something* about it that will put you on the path of resolving it? Maybe you're not. Be honest with yourself. Could you let go of the idea that you have to fix the situation, and accept yourself as is, at least for now?

This is a radical idea, certainly. My experience with

clients has shown that it has three positive effects, though. By releasing the pressure to need to change your ways, and accepting how things are, you reduce the overall friction in your life. While you'll still have the same things going on, they won't drain you so much because you won't see them as problematic anymore.

There's another possibility when giving something up on a trial basis. Experiment with the idea of letting go for a few days or weeks, consenting for a time to truly try on how it feels to relax the pressure on you about this. You may come to realize that giving it up *isn't* what you want. Because you haven't been operating from a place of self-judgment (self-hatred?), by removing the "must" from the equation you have now allowed yourself the space to be willing to approach what you've been putting off. The simple thought of letting go causes great conflict, so much so that you realize there is no way you're willing to forego doing this thing. You understand now that you have a choice, and you're unwilling to make the choice to let it go. This "whack upside the head" can be the inspiration for creating more options where there seemed to be none before, for designing a sturdy system, structure, support, or environment to follow through, delegating it to someone else, or just scheduling it in your calendar and doing it.

If, after all you've read, you've decided that what you've been putting off is necessary, and you're still not doing it, it's destructive procrastination. Refer to Part III of this book for ways to resolve destructive procrastination.

How urgent and important is it?

In his book, *The Seven Habits of Highly Effective People*, Stephen Covey relays a model for prioritizing. While Dr. Covey isn't the inventor of this model, his best-selling book has introduced it to many people. This model consists of a square divided into four quadrants:

(I) **Urgent and important** **ACTIVITIES:** • Crises • Pressing Problems • Deadline-driven projects	**(II)** **Not urgent but important** **ACTIVITIES:** • Prevention, Principle centered activities • Relationship Building • Recognizing new opportunities • Planning, recreation
(III) **Urgent and not important** **ACTIVITIES:** • Interruptions, some calls • Some mail, some reports • Some meetings • Proximate, pressing matters • Popular activities	**(IV)** **Not urgent and not important** **ACTIVITIES:** • Trivia, busy work • Some mail • Some phone calls • Time wasters • Pleasant activities

As you can see, importance relates to results. If

you've recognized a vision or purpose for yourself and if you've identified your values and want to live by them, having determined their priority in your life, then what is important are the tasks, projects, goals, and path you design to live in accordance with your vision, purpose, and values. It may be more important to you to have a low-stress, balanced lifestyle than to be a high-powered executive who travels around the world...or it may not.

Those things we often sense as pressing might be urgent rather than important. Covey writes, "Urgent matters are usually visible. They press on us; they insist on action. They're often popular with others. They're usually right in front of us. And often they are pleasant, easy, or fun to do. But so often they are unimportant!"

While on first glance Quadrant I, Urgent and Important, seems like it might be the appropriate place to be spending time, closer examination reveals that these are high stress situations that burn us out quickly. Instead, it's best to spend most of our time in Quadrant II, Not Urgent But Important. That's where we deal with the stuff that's important *before* it becomes a fire we have to put out right now.

While it's inevitable that you'll have to spend some time in Quadrant III and IV, by keeping a regular eye on the whole picture of your life, you can minimize your time there, and maximize it in II. Of course, there are probably a number of Quadrant IV items you're participating in that you can say goodbye to, while others can stay in your life and just be reduced (for example, fifteen to thirty minutes of television each day rather than three to four hours).

Take a close look at your to-do list. What are the consequences, in the grand scheme of your whole life, of doing or not doing each item? How well do they fit with the bigger picture of what you want your life to be about? Are doing these things truly the best use of your time? When you take a look back, will you be only relieved that you did something, or will you be proud of having done it?

If it's in Quadrants I or II, and it just isn't getting addressed over the period of months or years, it's destructive procrastination. It's cliché, but it works as an exercise to illustrate: if you were diagnosed with a terminal illness and given six months to live, you might not regret having a house that's less than tidy, or projects that you never finished, but you probably would regret not having health insurance or spending too little time with friends and loved ones.

Are you always on edge, tense, and worried about what you haven't done?

How much of your energy is being siphoned off by the constant stress of unfinished business? How much thought or time are you spending worrying about what isn't done? What kind of physical symptoms are you experiencing due to the strain that results from procrastination?

The short-term byproducts are bad enough, but research indicates that prolonged constant stress can strongly contribute to high blood pressure, heart conditions, ulcers, anxiety attacks, and worse. And it isn't any fun to live that way, anyway!

Make a closer inspection of your attitude, demeanor, and posture. Do you feel crabby and grouchy, or are you curt or short with others, particularly when there's something you should do but aren't doing (or are doing at the last minute)? Not only might this be affecting your health, it might also be affecting your relationships.

Do you believe you could accomplish more and be more relaxed if the pressure from the unfinished business was behind you? If my experience working with hundreds of people is any indication, the answer is likely to be a vigorous "Yes!"

Some of your stress may simply be due to unnecessary pressure you put on yourself based on unrealistic expectations (either yours or those of others). So that you can have a more objective perspective, it might be helpful to speak with friends, colleagues, or a coach about those expectations. Also, see the next section, below.

If your stress level is causing the level of your productivity, efficiency, and quality at work or attentiveness and performance in your personal life to be significantly cut, and you're not doing anything to address that, you can call it destructive procrastination.

Are you being reasonable in your expectations?

Perfectionism and its limiting constraints play into procrastination in a big way (as discussed in Chapter 2). When you examine your perspective more closely, how high are the standards you're setting for yourself?

Some people set the bar so high that it's very difficult to succeed. The standard is so unrealistically super-human that they prevent themselves from feeling like they've accomplished anything valuable, so they don't try at all. Perhaps you're using someone else's idea of good enough, and it's a rigorous and stringent yardstick to measure by, too much so for comfort—or effectiveness. "I'll do it when I have more time and energy," you say, knowing well that it's unlikely that the day you have *that* much time and energy will ever arrive.

Coupled with the focus on finishing the task, rather than starting it, very high standards result in self-sabotage. The fix for this is...ready? Lower your standards! Determine what is more reasonable and acceptable and experiment with reducing the benchmark by 30% to start with. Then concentrate on starting the individual pieces of the task—instead of finishing the project or goal.

If perfectionism is the biggest contributing problem, it may not be destructive procrastination, but simply a miscomprehension of how an outcome needs to look. Perhaps the task needn't be done at all, as it may only be a product of perfectionist tendencies. Refer to the other distinctions listed in this section to get a bigger picture.

On the other hand, if your expectations are practical,

realistic, and sensible, if you've checked your goal against your intentions and found them to be aligned with what you want in your life, if you've determined that this goal is necessary, prioritized and found this particular activity is important to you, timely, and appropriate, and you've still not accomplished your goal, you're looking at destructive procrastination.

Is it hurting your health?

Before you automatically answer yes, first ask yourself this: is your procrastination *actively and significantly* impairing your health or putting your health at *serious* risk?

Yes, you might be healthier losing those last ten or fifteen pounds, and it's possible you may extend your life a year or two by eating a few more fruits and veggies; you'll lower the incidence of plaque by flossing after every meal. It's not a bad idea to strive to make continual improvement. That doesn't mean not to do so is destructive procrastination. Why? There isn't a substantial negative impact on your physical condition or general health by not doing these things.

But there would be if you're smoking or engaging in some other "addictive" behavior such as overeating, drinking too much, taking drugs to help you function (when better habits would prevent the need to use them). Not taking timely action could have severe consequences. That's destructive, if you're unwilling to pay the price (see

Jack's story a little later in this chapter).

Having said that, it's a paradoxical but true statement that in order to be ready to change the habits you don't like, or the conditions you find wanting in yourself, you must first come to accept that they are part of being human. Learning to be compassionate with yourself for not being perfect is an absolutely huge step toward the kind of change that's sustainable enough to be transformative.

Recognizing and laughing at your own humanity doesn't make you weak. It does the opposite, making you more flexible to "dance" with what life throws you, more calm-headed to be able to see benefits and options where you formerly saw only the negative, more clear-minded and focused on the intention behind your goals so that in the end you've achieved something of value rather than a hollow accomplishment.

There are other health-related areas where procrastination may be destructive. If you know you have, or may be developing, a condition which is a substantial threat to your health and you're not taking action, it could be critical, possibly even fatal. If you're verging on obesity (as are over 50% of the American population), while it might not be immediately life-threatening, the incidence of many diseases are associated with obesity. If you haven't embarked on any kind of exercise and/or diet restructuring plan, this would be considered destructive procrastination, depending on your other life situations, degree of obesity, and other factors.

Many people avoid beginning an exercise program because they think it will be too vigorous, painful, time-consuming, boring, or inconvenient. There are, though, so many easy and painless ways to incorporate exercise. I know this from personal experience, because I'm not a person who likes to exercise. I've experimented a lot in this area, both on my own and with my clients, with excellent results. Walking your own—or a neighbor's—pet, dancing (alone, in the dark, to music that's irresistibly leg-twitchingly, arm flailingly danceable), cleaning house while blasting lively music, doing silly aerobics with your kids, and playing Frisbee are a lot more fun than what we call "exercise," yet still qualify to help get you or keep you in shape.

No matter what, you always have a choice about your health (and much else in life, for that matter). You can simply choose to not take action and accept that you've made this choice, along with its consequences.

I knew Jack years ago, and don't know whether he's even still around or not. Jack was a diabetic, and he drank and smoked and ate rich, sweet foods. He knew the risks full well. For years the consequences didn't seem so severe, but he knew there would come a time when he'd have to "pay the piper." To Jack, though, the idea of living without enjoyment of liquor, cigars, and sweets wasn't much of a life. During the time I knew him, when he was in his mid-fifties, he lost part of his left foot through diabetic complications. Although he wasn't happy about it, when he re-evaluated his lifestyle, he came to the same conclusion. You may think he was stupid or crazy or lacked discipline. I knew him pretty well, and I couldn't say he was any of those things. Who am I to judge someone else's values or impose my values on them? He was entitled to live his life as he liked, and he did. Just because you and I don't share those same values and preferences doesn't mean he was wrong or misguided. For me, Jack has become a hero of sorts, hewing to his own standards and lifestyle, regardless what the rest of us think, not beset by self-doubt and self-loathing.

You probably know people who haven't given up alcohol or smoking. Most of them have not made peace with themselves about it, but some have. Do you have friends or family who, in spite of the health ramifications, are sanguine that they will always be thirty or forty pounds overweight because they delight so much in food and eating? Rather than their enjoyment in life being ruined by guilt, it has been enhanced, not by giving up smoking, drinking, or fattening foods, but simply by accepting their choices and enjoying those things. Ironically, enjoyment in life is statistically related to lower levels of disease and death. That's something to think about!

Put a tick mark in the destructive procrastination column if procrastination is *actively and significantly* impairing your health or putting your health at serious risk.

Is it truly preventing you from experiencing the success you want?

What are your intentions for your life? Have you created any, or are you living life by default? So many of my clients and workshop participants would love to have more fabulous lives, but they don't really have a good idea of what that means to them. Since they don't have any destination, they can't even create a map to get there.

I'm not referring to a life of what you *don't* want, but rather what you'd love to have in your life on a sustainable every day basis. What would make life more fulfilling and satisfactory for you? This may seem too broad of a scope for a book on procrastination, but actually, it couldn't be more relevant.

Without creating a clear vision of the life they'd like, most people get bogged down in activities and habits that they think they should be doing, or they accept responsibilities or ways of being that don't fit them. These things are a continual drain on them, whittling away at not only their energy, but their drive, purpose, and contribution. This kind of drain fuels procrastination, big time.

If your procrastination bugaboo is just a niggling annoyance, a form of self-pressure that is productivity dampening (but not really necessary), it's productive or neutral. If it's genuinely a barrier to living your life on your own terms, fully and unrestrainedly, label it destructive.

Chapter 8
When Procrastination Affects Others

Are others being hurt or jeopardized by your lack of action?

Evaluate the impact on others in any instance where you're not getting things done in as timely a manner as you think you should. Is there an impact on other people or just you? How significant is that impact, both as perceived by you, *and* by them? How much is real versus imagined on your part? How much is real versus imagined on theirs? What are the consequences to them? Are there organizations you've taken on responsibilities for and are not following through with? What bearing does that have on that organization's ability to fulfill their initiatives, events, and mission?

This is a procrastination indication measure that could really go either way. Are you truly making enemies (you may be!) or are you just imagining you could be?

Have other people perceived your lack of attention or completion to be of concern for them? Have you already heard about it? You may or may not know exactly why they're concerned. The best way to find out is to ask. Have some conversations with those people involved, especially those upon whom your delaying might have the most significant effect. They'll feel better about both you and the situation if you show them that you want to understand things from their point of view and address them accordingly. On one hand, you may get additional information and impetus (in the form of motivation to reduce the likelihood of the relationship further souring) required to stimulate you to complete things.

On the other hand, maybe other people involved aren't at all concerned. Unless someone has specifically indicated to you they're upset, angry, or disappointed in you, you won't know until you ask.

Must co-workers or other volunteers do your work or cover for you to meet deadlines, cover responsibilities, or complete tasks? Are your children being put at a real and significant disadvantage? Are your friends insulted or incensed because of your lack of follow through? If so, it's destructive, and it's costing you deeply.

Don't be guilt-tripped, though

Not all the displeasure of others is created equal. Are there situations in which others are simply guilt-tripping you into doing what they want, for their own reasons or values (which you may not share)? They may be pushing you toward expectations that are too high for you, or in directions that don't fit you. You're responsible for your own path and your own feelings, not anyone else's. If someone is trying to manipulate you into doing things that aren't in your interest, it's wiser to decline.

As usual, an ounce of prevention is worth a pound of cure. It would have been even smarter to not accept a responsibility or expectation in the first place! If you're in an established relationship or circumstance that isn't serving you, I'm not giving you permission to be irresponsible, insensitive, egotistical, or unkind. If you're procrastinating on setting a date to get married to the wrong person, don't set the date, but have a heart-to-heart discussion about the relationship and where it's going. Treat your fiancé with respect and compassion. Treat everyone with respect and compassion, come to think of it!

Maybe your home office space is pretty cluttered, but you know where everything is, can find things quickly, and it doesn't bother you that it isn't tidy and attractive— but it bugs your significant other, or your kids. Instead of just dragging your feet, why not have a negotiating conversation about it? Maybe that could be your space alone, and the agreement is that the door is kept shut and you'll be neat and tidy and organized everywhere else in the house? That, by the way, is how we deal with my husband's office in my own house.

Jill had been working on her doctoral study in economics for the last two years, haltingly, and she'd lost her enthusiasm for it, not to mention an entire career spent in it. Meanwhile, her husband Tom was supporting both of them. This was part of the career path and income plan they'd made a couple of years earlier, but Jill had recently realized it no longer fit her. Even though she was gifted in mathematics and had an easy grasp of policy, after a master's degree and working for a government agency, the glamour was gone. She was really bored by economics and frustrated by government policies. She wanted to work as a lobbyist. She no longer found economics interesting or exciting as she had five or ten years ago, and saw her future as dull and stifling if she continued on the same path. She didn't want to disappoint Tom, but more than that, she didn't want to hate her work life. When she finally admitted this to Tom, he was upset, angry even, just as she thought he would be. "How could you throw away all you've been building toward?" he asked. Through continuing conversations, though, addressing the matter with Tom, she politely and caringly refused to buy into any manipulation or pressure. Within a few weeks Jill and Tom had a tentative new plan in place that they could both feel comfortable with, and an agreement to revisit the plan every year.

Through my experience with clients, as well as my own personal experience, you'll have much greater satisfaction, and possibly higher respect of those very same people, if you stand your ground and kindly, respectfully refuse to buy in to their ideas of how and who you should be.

Beyond guilt trips and misplaced expectations, you are responsible for the consequences of your actions, or lack thereof. Sometimes you'll be successful, and other times it won't work out quite as well, but that's okay. The important thing is to be aware and make the effort to act accordingly, to end destructive procrastination when it's pissing off and disappointing people who matter.

Is your performance suffering?

By performance, I'm referring to the various responsibilities you may have. They may include those of:

- Professional, business owner, or employee
- money handler
- homeowner
- volunteer
- board member
- husband or wife (or significant other)
- mother or father
- son or daughter
- friend or colleague

Are there one or more of these areas where your performance is suffering significantly? What results are forfeit because you haven't taken action? How effective are you in the roles you've assumed, and what positions, assets, opportunities, relationships, or reputation might you lose if you continue to put things off? When you have obligations that affect other people, there are costs to you and them. Is there something significant you're going to lose, like your business, your job, your house, or your savings? What about your marriage, custody of your kids, or treasured friendships?

While you can't be expected to be a superhero all the time at every one of these, it is possible to have all these bases covered well enough most of the time. Could we all do better in any one of them? Sure, but there is a point of diminishing returns where putting much more into any one area could negatively affect the rest of them.

A balance over time is what you're looking for. There will be periods when you must pay more attention to your business or career, or your children might be going through a difficult time and need more attention. It may be in the best interests of your marriage or relationship to invest a bigger chunk of your time and attention, diverting some from your job or volunteer duties before it's too late. At those times, it helps to accept that you're not going to have daily or weekly "balance" while you concentrate on resolving or stabilizing those situations. The strategy is to plan and work toward the time when you can sustain an acceptable "performance" level in that area so that you can ease off there a bit and apply yourself to the other areas in your life.

You may be so focused on your work that you're skimping on attention to your family life, marriage, friendships, and/or volunteer activities. On the other hand, you may be putting effort into all areas except making your business the success you want it to be.

In any of these situations, there are conflicting desires or commitments at work. The energy of one intention, for instance to be successful in your career, may interfere or conflict with another commitment or desire to spend as much time with your kids or significant other as you'd like. You might really want a more successful business or career, but that requires really putting yourself out there and possibly facing rejection or failure.

The upshot is that something is getting ignored, or at least getting the short end of the stick, and your responsibilities in that area are costing you in some way. Determine what those specific costs are, and their level of "expense" to you. Whether the expense is relatively small or pretty large, are you willing to continue "paying" it (you may be! This might truly be a viable option in many situations), or is it truly more than you're willing to continue to tolerate? If it's more than you're really willing to pay (regardless of "shoulds"!) and you're still doing nothing to fix it, you guessed it, it's destructive procrastination.

Is your job or marriage being at risk a good thing or a bad thing?

For a number of my clients, this is a pretty loaded question. I've had many clients come to me because they procrastinate on taking action, fulfilling the responsibilities, or making decisions regarding their jobs, businesses, or marriages. They may be hanging on to positions, careers, businesses, or relationships that are no longer serving them. In this way, they are playing what I call the Procrastination Abdication Game, relinquishing their control (and responsibility) until things come to a head.

While it may feel like something of a surprise when things suddenly blow up, they've been brewing for some time, usually months or years. My clients have often found that these transitions and endings, while they are difficult, help nudge, push, or jolt them to make changes that they knew they needed to make but were simply afraid to risk. They didn't understand the risk was just as great, if not greater, by not addressing what wasn't working. The downside is that they may have lost a lot in the process of playing the Procrastination Abdication Game, such as money, reputation, general satisfaction, and something that can never be replaced: time.

The Procrastination Abdication Game may be disastrous: you may lose a job or position that you cherish. A relationship or marriage to someone that you dearly love may be irreparably, irretrievably harmed.

How close to bailing on you are your clients, your spouse, your boss? How much does that matter to you? You'll know that your procrastination is destructive if the answers are, "very," or "getting close," and in your heart of hearts, it's not what you want. If you don't know how ready they are, ask! If you care about staying in your job or marriage, open the lines of communication and find out.

Is it costing you more money than you're willing to pay?

Unless you're pretty rich, you strongly prefer not to waste money and ruin (or further degrade) your credit record, right?

There are many ways you may be incurring financial costs through procrastination. The most obvious include paying penalties and late fees when you fail to pay bills on time. By doing that you're also, of course, lowering your credit rating.

When you don't make progress in creating a plan to pay off your debt and budget your spending, you're paying big bucks in debt financing—and failing to put money away for the future. How many more years will you need to work before you can retire, if ever? Perhaps you've even given up on the idea. One of my clients, in the process of taking a closer look at how debt was affecting her life, paid off $60,000 of debt in just over six months. It was an extreme challenge for her, but it was well worth it to her to no longer have that burden—it had been too painful, too inconvenient, too distracting.

I've had clients who had put off de-cluttering their files, and through working with me they found hundreds of dollars in unused traveler's checks, gift certificates, and un-cashed checks (one for $90,000!). Other clients found business proposals they hadn't completed, viable prospects for new accounts they hadn't followed up on, income-generating ideas and opportunities they'd wanted to follow-up on but which had gotten lost in a pile, refund and rebate forms they never filled out and sent in, insurance reimbursements they'd had delayed in acting on…and the list goes on.

Whether it's missing out on discounts on the things you're already going to buy, having to pay bank fees because you put off reconciling your checking account and are overdrawn, or not acting before prices go up, all (or at least some) of that money could be going toward something you'd really like to have or experience in your life.

Putting off becoming somewhat educated about saving and investing means that you may very well not have money for "rainy days," such as medical emergencies, accidents, or some sudden and unforeseen misfortune. I'm not even remotely suggesting that you should live such a careful life that you take no risks, nor that you become overly concerned with catastrophic possibilities. I'm just recommending (strongly) that while you have faith that everything will happen, as it should, in the general sense, you are financially prepared for a few thousand dollars worth of unanticipated expenses. You may have experienced how much more costly (as well as frustrating, difficult, and upsetting) things are to fix or handle when you haven't previously given thought to or acted on making provisions or created some financial reserve.

So, how much of your money is going down the proverbial toilet? Is it enough to matter to you?

It may not be. Don't expect that you'll ever fit your own model of perfect (or even close). We all make mistakes, we're all (well, most of us, including me) sometimes late with a payment or bill, we all occasionally spend more than we need to or should. The question is whether your level of dollar drain is sustainable and endurable, or not. If not, you'll want to deal with this destructive procrastination.

Is there a moderate to strong risk of accident or injury to yourself or others?

Are the steel rims of your tires showing through? Do you have a ladder leaning against the house that could fall over? Are there flammable materials (piles of papers, magazines, newspapers, or boxes) near any heat sources? Are you delaying fixing frayed electrical wiring or a step that is loose, broken, or weak?

Again, moderate to strong risk of accident/injury, as opposed to slight, is important in using this determinant of positive vs. neutral vs. destructive procrastination. Another way to say it would be possible vs. probable.

Sometimes we postpone repairs because they're expensive, or the one repair might necessitate another and it feels like we're getting deeper and deeper into renovation or restoration, like it will never end, or will become more than we want to or can handle. But how much more will it cost you if you have to go to the hospital for a broken arm because you tripped over the carpeting at the door that's needed repair for the last couple of months? How much more would it cost you if it were someone else, someone who ended up suing you?

How much time and money will be lost if a fire consumes some of your home because you've put off cleaning out your dryer vent lines or a dying tree you've been ignoring falls on your house?

If there is any structural reconstruction necessary anywhere, any electrical appliance, outlet, switch, or socket that is faulty, or anything which affects the safe operation of your vehicles, and you're putting off mending any of it, it's destructive procrastination. Trust me—my dad died in an electrical fire.

It may not be only your own safety that's in danger, but also your loved ones, guests, colleagues, or customers. Please read Part III of this book, and immediately deal with any tasks that fall into this category of destructive procrastination.

So, is it productive, destructive, or neutral?

By now you should have a very good grasp of which procrastination situations are desirable, which you can forget about for the moment, and which need to be fixed right away. I'll make an educated guess that some fit into each category.

For those situations that you've concluded are productive procrastination...celebrate! Congratulations and good work for managing your efforts better than you'd thought you'd been. I hope you feel more lighthearted and confident in your own wisdom, and that removing the self-criticism for putting those things off allows for more energy to pursue those things you really care about. Doesn't it feel fantastic?

There is, of course, the other side of the coin. What turned out to be destructive procrastination? How do you stop? Turn the page for Part III of this book, where you'll find powerful strategies and techniques that get to the root of procrastination and provide practical, simple structure to get things done with less struggle and in less time.

Part III

**Procrastination Elimination:
Dissolving Destructive Procrastination**

Chapter 9
It's Real, It's Ugly...Now What?

So, there's no way around it, it's really procrastination, the bad, destructive kind. Any way you slice it, there's little evidence you can come up with to support that what you're procrastinating on is wisely put off. Blithely crossing this off your list unaccomplished is simply not an option. Now what?

According to Piers Steel, a procrastination researcher at the University of Calgary in Canada, "we tend to favor tasks that are more pleasant in the short-term even if they are detrimental to ourselves in the long-term. Second, the more intrinsically unpleasant is a task, the more likely we are to avoid doing it. These outcomes are intuitively obvious and, in fact, they are so dependably replicated that they can be considered 'laws' of behavior." (The Nature of Procrastination, University of Calgary, 2003)

So the more worth our while in the short term the task is the more likely we are to do it, and the more boring, difficult, or uncomfortable a task is, the more we put it off. DUH! That's what I call an astute observation of the obvious!

What isn't as obvious to many people who consider themselves procrastinators is that they'll have more success in accomplishment if they understand one simple concept:

Align your short-term rewards as closely as you can with your long-term objectives

Have you ever noticed how when your taxes are due and you might have to pay penalties and interest charges, your long-term objective of getting your taxes done aligns with your short-term objective of avoiding those penalties and late fees? Do you remember, as a kid, how the long-term objective of being able to go out and play with your friends aligned with the short-term objective of getting your room cleaned up or finishing your homework so your mom would let you out to play? As any situation either gets closer to a negative consequence or a positive payoff, your in-the-minute intentions start to work in concert with your broader goals. While you may have tried this before, there are approaches to this that require less friction, effort, and discipline than you might think. Would you like methods that didn't involve slogging through the dread and exhorted you to "just do it?"

This section of the book presents a variety of techniques designed to help you do just that.

It's immensely helpful to understand the mechanism of procrastination first, so you know what you're dealing with. Self-observation in the moment, suspending judgment for the time being, is where we start.

The mechanics of procrastination

Say, for example, that, like millions of other people, you have a desire to get more organized. You're tired of being frustrated and annoyed by the appearance of, distraction by, and efficiency-reducing effects of clutter that has been accumulating for too long.

At the same time as that desire arises, other desires and sensations accompany it: it will be difficult, it will take too long, you don't have the time to devote to it, and once it's done you'll have to maintain it which is also daunting, etc. There may be a host of other competing commitments, too, such as that you want it to be perfect, but you know it probably won't come out that way, so why even start? Or you'd love to have a house like your super-organized friend, but you don't want to be as uptight or rigid as her or him, or you've come to label yourself in a way that implies you can never accomplish that.

None of these thoughts are sharply detailed in your mind. They're all a jumble, but they produce a sense of inner conflict that feels uncomfortable.

Then, automatically, without really thinking about it, your attention simply switches from your intention to get organized to something else (anything else!). Perhaps you suddenly remember that you had meant to call a friend, or do the laundry, or like 67% of the people in my survey, read your e-mail. Maybe you find yourself drifting to your Procrastination Location (in front of the refrigerator, the computer, or the television are the most popular places).

A vital first step in procrastination termination is to become familiar with that very moment in which your energy is first directed toward a goal or task and then gets sapped by inner conflict, leading to the substitution of some other direction for your energy. This is "the moment of truth" and the place where your old pattern will begin to change on the path toward abolishing destructive procrastination.

How about a little experiment? Read the exercise below, put the book down for a minute, and see what happens in the interim.

Exercise: Procrastination Confrontation

Imagine that as soon as you put down this book you're going to tackle one of the tasks you've been putting off. Think about the task and what you would do. Imagine yourself getting up and going to where you would take action on the task, and starting to work on it. Now watch what your mind does. Put the book down now and play with this exercise.

Okay, you're back. Did your mind ricochet off the task into some other thought, activity, or other must-do to-do? Did some competing desires, intentions, or beliefs pop up? Or maybe you actually followed through on the task. If so, fabulous! You're already experiencing some success. Another possibility is that you just kept reading and thought you'd do the exercise at some later time (if at all). That's part of the procrastination pattern, but that's okay, you're getting familiar with how it works. You've just noticed the resistance that's a hallmark of the pattern.

Part of George's job responsibilities included

completing sales reports each Friday. His boss was unhappy with him because George rarely got the reports completed and just guestimated, leading to inaccuracies. That caused problems for his boss. George knew he had to buckle down, but when he sat in front of his computer monitor with a spreadsheet in front of him, he needed to get some order information for it, so he accessed his e-mail program. He found himself working on e-mail twenty minutes later, not even realizing how much time had passed and that he'd never even finished looking for the information he needed to complete the report. E-mail was a huge distraction for him. Isn't it for most of us!

When George and I started discussing how to get on track with the reports, some competing desires immediately surfaced. As a salesperson for a beverage company, George made his money and his mandated targets by making sales, not filling out reports. He resented having to take the time to complete them and resisted doing them, even though he knew it was part of the job. It wasn't what he was good at or enjoyed, he said. It didn't feel like a priority to him, and he felt it didn't contribute to his or the company's bottom line. His boss had explained to him that the sales department needed to send the weekly numbers so the production department could accurately forecast their projected need for resources.

Going deeper, George's intellectual story was that he believed that compiling the weekly sales data required that he focus less on sales. As a result, he wouldn't then meet his targets, a thought more displeasing than having his boss call him on the carpet for not completing a lousy report. At the emotional level, though, George was facing what felt like a loss of control, something that felt vaguely threatening. George was stuck in resistance and discomfort.

The enemy is not discomfort, not even fear

Remember, you've got decades of built-up habit that helps you avoid any place where you sense discomfort may lurk. You're very adept at steering clear of them, even if, ironically, the resulting procrastination is itself uncomfortable; you're just used to experiencing it (the devil you know is better than the devil you don't). Procrastination is simply a coping mechanism, a way of resisting that uneasiness. The impulse to steer clear of anything that feels bad is deeply ingrained, practiced dozens of times each day over the months, years, and decades of your life. Paradoxically, the only way around is *through*. More about that in the next chapter. For the moment, let's get a little deeper understanding of what we're attempting to dodge in our Procrastination Machinations.

Taking a look at what you're aware of as this inner conflict starts arising, you may notice a few things, such as fear of failure, avoiding tedium, or difficulty, or even just a general sense of "ickiness." (Check out the list in Chapter 1) These are true and valid, but they are not the source or generation point of the procrastination. Underneath each of these is the inclination to run away from anything that could lead to feeling overwhelmed. It may just look like discomfort if we examine it intellectually, but if you keep exploring it and asking yourself questions about it, you'll eventually get to the sense you might lose control, or be unable to bear what comes up.

You may recall that at the beginning of the book I mentioned spindle cells. These spindle cells, which process emotion, are pretty scarce when we're tiny, multiplying as we grow into childhood. Because we didn't have them early on, we went into overwhelm easily. It was a very scary place, and we want to avoid it at all costs because it feels like we're being destroyed.

As we grew a little older, we started to recognize the signs of possible impending overwhelm and our intelligent homo sapiens brains developed strategies to bypass or evade it. We learned to develop a variety of alternatives to being overwhelmed, procrastination being one of those alternatives. A pattern was established. This pattern underlies your adult behavior until you recognize and accept it, and then begin to change the pattern.

When you resort to the procrastination habit, you're under a mistaken illusion that you can escape the accompanying feeling of inner turmoil, that you can circumvent it. What's really going on is that we've created this big monster (overwhelm) in our heads that prompts us to do something else (anything else!) in order to avoid even seeing the monster (feeling the overwhelm), because we believe the monster is really scary. Any time we have to do anything non-fun, tedious, requiring going outside a comfort zone, difficult, complicated, demanding, or taxing in some way, even though we're unaware of it, our faculties recognize the pattern that we've experienced before which is a precursor to overwhelm, and we automatically evade going there by shifting our focus elsewhere.

Unfortunately, that monster continues knocking at the door of your awareness, distracting you even while you're trying to ignore it. You think you've put it aside, but it persists and saps your attention and concentration, it nags ever so quietly at you, continually requesting that you open the door to it. Try to disregard it as you might, it still has power over you.

The ironic thing is that the monster is a holograph. Because of the resistance to even acknowledging that there's a monster there, which seems like it's a big, hairy, snarling, carnivorous beast ready to seize and devour us at its first opportunity, we steer clear of anything that's uncomfortable. That's just a way we learned to cope with it, but it's no longer an effective or productive method.

We've developed an entire culture of pursuing comfort and avoiding as much discomfort as possible. Now, that's not a bad thing on its own, but together with our normal upbringing, it's fostered a very strong motivation to remain within the confines of the comfort zone, and has made a real villain of discomfort.

We've allowed this discomfort to stop us in our tracks, and procrastination is the result. Much of the research that's been done on procrastination has been on college students. That's not only because they're an easy target for academic researchers but because procrastination is epidemic among college students, so much so that many colleges and universities have counseling programs specifically geared to that problem.

Two studies were done in Belgium and the Netherlands and published in 2002. One revealed that procrastination was closely related to a lack of perseverance, that is, the inability to complete projects. The researchers believed this explained a large part of the well-documented relationship between conscientiousness and procrastination. In the second study, students were followed up during eleven weeks before their exams, providing their study intentions, actual behavior, the reasons why they failed to enact their intentions, and the perceived impact of studying on their final grade. It's no surprise that the data revealed that all students tend to postpone the bulk of their study activities to the last week before an exam, and that procrastinators postponed more of their intentions, mainly because of fun alternatives, but did not intend to study less or later. Actually, they formulated more intentions earlier, seeming to compensate for their vulnerability. Procrastinators emerged as highly motivated students who lack the ability to ward off temptations and distractions during their studying activities. It's so much more tempting to do the fun stuff than study—now isn't that a surprise!

The gift of fear and resistance

There's another way to view what we've perceived as discomfort: that it's simply useful information. Whether there's a fear of failure that comes up, a fear of success (or delayed failure, as described by Neil Forte in *The Now Habit*), fear of loss of control, of change, or isolation or rejection, the information that precedes that fear or unease doesn't need to be used to prevent us from moving forward, but can instead be utilized to help us prepare for our success.

A number of years ago I heard an interview with a woman who, at the time, held the world record for number of sky diving jumps. The interviewer asked her, "You're not afraid?" She replied, "I'm scared as hell, but that's what helps keep me safe. I use my fear to help me prepare as thoroughly as possible." That was a new perspective for me, and I use this story with clients all the time. It's a paradigm shift: instead of allowing the fear to stop her, she channeled it into a productive use. How can they productively channel their fears to help them excel rather than hold them back?

Veronica suffered through a nasty divorce and was now going through a contentious custody battle with her ex. Meanwhile, her financial situation is a mess, and her new live-in boyfriend isn't contributing much to their common household expenses. Veronica had been in a bad car accident a year and a half earlier. Her neck and shoulder cause her a lot of pain, so much that she needs to lie down for a few hours every day, preventing her from working any kind of regular job. She's been pulling money out of savings to stay in her current house. She knows she needs to cut her expenses by moving to a less expensive place, but she hasn't actively been looking. Even though she and her boyfriend are squabbling a lot and she admits the relationship is pretty much over, she's been putting off the crucial conversation.

Veronica fears being alone and being destitute. Who wouldn't in her situation? She's afraid she'll end up in a trailer park forever, in debt the rest of her days, will lose visitation rights with her kids, as well as their respect, and will never recover anything like the comfortable lifestyle she used to have.

Rather than shying away from Veronica's fears, and letting them overwhelm her, we use them to strategize, create plans, and take actions. She worries about how hard it will be, and comes to realize it won't be any harder than what she's been dealing with for the past year and a half.

Within two weeks Veronica has looked at a few apartments, so far none of them appealing but she's continuing to ask around and explore possibilities. She's updated her resume and has been in contact with friends, family, and former co-workers to find a job. She's now legally disabled, and there are positions available that will bring reasonable income, and more empowerment than the disability payments she's been scraping by with. She's been thinking about the talk she'll soon have with her boyfriend. A month later she has moved, without her boyfriend, and she's been going on interviews.

Our fears are there to protect us, to warn us of the possibility of failure and to alert us to what we might need to prepare for. Through our fears, we can become clear on the risks of any particular decision or action. Then, we can do what we need to mitigate the risk as much as we can. There is a point, though, where that risk is managed as much as it can be managed, but it's not gone. It's time to ask yourself whether you are willing and able to take that risk or not.

Chapter 10
Slaying the Inner Dragon

Most books on procrastination advise you to be disciplined, push through the discomfort, or "just do it," using tips and tricks. There is a common theme that runs through them that regards the discomfort as dreaded, distasteful, and either to be avoided or swept under the rug. That's one way of overcoming procrastination, though it takes lots of consistent willpower, energy, and a good deal of struggle. Between you and me, we both know it's not sustainable.

Experience with clients tells me that you don't have to put all your eggs in the willpower basket. You don't have to endure, struggle, "survive" the discomfort. I believe that the "discomfort" is an illusion and is followed by what is simply a patterned avoidance response. My experience working with clients, leading workshops, and training hundreds of coaches has shown that when you stop running and avoiding, what you actually experience, once you get past resistance to experiencing it, is...are you ready? Nothing! That's right, nothing.

Physicists tell us that everything is energy, in different forms. The paper you're reading this on (or the computer screen) is a form of energy. The clothes you're wearing are a form of energy. A simplified explanation is that while each form of energy seems like a different thing, it's really just different "flavors" of energy. Your thoughts, perceptions, and emotions are no exception. Energy is always in movement, always in flux, always transforming itself, just as the energy of the sun is transformed into photosynthesis, and that is transformed, eventually, into the fruits, vegetables, and grains we eat.

When you perceive anything, a set of energy patterns are recognized and automatically compared to previous experiences and patterns. That's how your brain works. Whenever it recognizes a pattern associated with anything which has previously been in some way scary or uncomfortable—and even boredom has its threatening side—to your intellect, it provokes "The Security Threat Response": a survival mechanism that definitely has its benefits. Your body responds with a cascade of chemicals that ready you for action. They prompt you to run faster across the street if a car turns a corner too speedily and might hit you, they warn you not to walk alone into a dark alley, they advise caution and restraint when you're faced with a challenge you're not sure you can handle, but that you must deal with. You somehow access some knowledge about what you have to do. There isn't much, if any, thought or decision-making before you act. That's the Inner Guidance System at work.

When you can fight or flee, you dissipate the energy that The Security Threat Response generates. Freezing, as you probably know, is another option, but it usually doesn't allow for the same dissipation of energy as fighting or fleeing does. This energy, and the sensations that accompany it, don't just go away, they stay there, and because it feels threatening in some way, we resist any focus on it. Sometimes this results in trauma. On a lesser scale, it triggers procrastination. When you avoid fully processing the energy and sensations generated they remain a prisoner in your awareness, so to speak, banging on the bars for your attention, persisting even while you're doing other things. You can still "hear" that banging, and it disturbs your ability to function effectively. Some things bang louder and more persistently than others, and the result can be some pretty non-productive behavior (and, more destructively, addictive behaviors).

That imprisoned energy pattern just hangs out there, at times just being an annoyance, at other times really festering while waiting to be processed. The Security Threat Response itself is working overtime. It tells you those sensations and that energy are scary, and warns you to avoid allowing yourself to fully experience them. But that is all you'd be doing—processing the energy and sensations associated with it—not getting caught up in stories or hijacked by emotions, which is what we usually do, and allows us to continue to resist.

The Security Threat Response is there to protect you, but it's like an overprotective Jewish grandmother who is always worrying and predicting catastrophes. "Don't do it!" it screams, "You'll never come back alive!" But the threat is imagined. It's like a hologram.

When I first started experimenting with this technique, it reminded me of the Star Trek episodes in which crewmembers were being killed by enemies who turned out to be holograms. Those crew members where shot with a phazer, stabbed with a knife, or engaged in hand-to-hand combat, but they actually died of heart attacks or broken necks rather than wounds, because their brains influenced their bodies into believing they were fatally injured. Once the rest of the crew understood and believed that the bad guys were not a real, physical manifestation, the enemy holograms completely lost the power to harm the crew.

While The Security Threat Response is holding us back, our intellect tells us to move forward, so we feel like we have one foot on the gas pedal and the other on the brake, spinning our wheels at high speed but going nowhere—and we're drained by it. We try to rationalize and explain and give reasons why we're procrastinating. All that stuff is just window dressing. That's when it's time to invite our Inner Guidance System into action. Our intellect is an extremely useful thing, but when we're limiting our experience to it alone, we're missing a lot of other vital information and experience. Have you ever noticed how the most successful people in business, sports, and art seem to utilize not only their minds, but also their bodies and their spirits?

We've mostly been socialized into rigorous and strict use of the mind, and conditioned out of utilizing the body and the spirit. If we have an ache or pain, we don't listen to our bodies and adjust our habits, schedules, ergonomics, or lifestyles. We don't allow the sensation fully, but ignore or resist it or take an aspirin to quiet it and keep on working. And then we pay heavily for it later through chronic disease that would have been preventable if we had only listened. We question and doubt most of our spiritual inklings and experiences as they're not empirical enough—we have no proof. Yet, how many times have you ignored your intuition about something and then deeply regretted it? We mostly distrust any gut sensations because we can't explain them, but when allowed and explored, they are fabulous at finding answers for us, and surprisingly quick at re-energizing us for action.

Barbara Jean needs to earn some income. She and her husband agree that they both need to work a few more years before they both retire. The business she started a year ago hasn't taken off, and doesn't look like it's going to. She has to find work, but she isn't doing much about it.

As we talk, Barbara Jean realizes that resentment is one of the reasons she hasn't put much effort into job-hunting. She's at an age where she really doesn't want to work anymore. It's useful to recognize and acknowledge that resentment is there. It's a good first step, but she still needs to work, so we still need to explore further.

I ask Barbara Jean if the resentment is making her feel tense right now. It is, and the tension is located in her sternum, where her ribs meet. That's the sensation and energy we're looking for. I take her straight into it, right down into the thick of it. At first, it seems too scary for her to face, so we back off, but soon she is ready to try again. She drops her attention squarely into the uncomfortable sensation in her chest. It's tight, pulsing, and heavy like a big black bowling ball. I ask her to find a way into it, into the very center of the ball. At first there is no way in—a form of resistance. I ask her to take a deep inhale and then exhale while looking for or creating an opening. It works, she's in. She finds blackness, nothing. A feeling of hopelessness surfaces, and she feels tears ready to come. I ask her for another deep breath, and to not resist but be curious about whatever there is to experience. After a moment or two, Barbara Jean explains that she had lost a job she loved just prior to the 9/11 terrorist attacks. After that national tragedy, the nation took stock and the economy took a dip. Barbara Jean looked for a new position for months, with no luck, and felt hopeless.

As I direct her to continue her focus on this dark interior place, to allow it and observe it, she relaxes. She begins to notice some light at the edge, and follows it, coming out to a wooded clearing, where she sees a lively child of about six. The child asks a lot of questions and seems pretty fearless—she recognizes the child as herself, as the part of her that is still curious, exploring, intrepid, a guide reminding her that she didn't have to be held hostage by age, previous experience, and uncomplimentary beliefs. Barbara Jean was ready to have some interesting internal dialogue with this little girl.

Less than a month later, Barbara Jean has been offered two good positions with different firms and has taken the better one. She is re-acclimating to the commute and the rigors of a full time job, and is enjoying applying her energy, intelligence, and experience in the job, and receiving fair pay in exchange.

The exercise you're about to read (and hopefully try for yourself) helps you reconnect the body and spirit, and brings the mind into balance with them.

When you fully experience what comes up for you, rather than resisting by default, a few things usually happen:

- Either the energy, which starts out as scary, intense, and seemingly overwhelming, dissipates, evaporates, or just disappears, or
- The energy transforms into a calm, peaceful, serene, sensation. And then,
- You're no longer feeling stuck or uncomfortable, but instead are enthusiastic and ready to tackle what you've been putting off. It no longer feels like a struggle, but instead feels easy and inviting.

Sometimes you'll discover layers of sensation, other times the energy may move from one place to another, on occasion moving again or returning to its original spot.

The following exercise may at first seem strange, woo-woo, or discomfort evoking, or you may find your attention being diverted (this is one form of resistance). If you find you're getting caught up in an emotion or when your mind starts running away with you, don't judge yourself or this process. Simply bring your attention back to where the most intense and uncomfortable energy exists in your body.

You'll use this exercise at that moment in between the desire to accomplish your task and your inclination to procrastinate on it.

Exercise:

Dissolving Overwhelm

Use this technique when you are on the verge of putting something off. Stop yourself at the moment you're about to put off a task. Don't judge yourself, but simply observe any discomfort. There is something you want to avoid feeling. At its most basic, this is the fear of being overwhelmed.

Invite your Inner Guidance System to weigh in on anything you're making a decision about or delaying action on. Notice, in the moment, as you're about to put something off, and observe that there is some discomfort. There is something you want to avoid feeling. At its most basic, this is the fear of being overwhelmed.

At the moment you notice this, rather than allowing your focus to shift to something else, simply sit quietly with your eyes closed and allow yourself to sense the discomfort rather than resist it. You'll probably notice some tension and resistance. This is entirely normal. Allow yourself to notice and feel that tension and resistance. It's very likely that it's showing up as tightness, pressure, throbbing, burning, heaviness, swirling sensation, or other unpleasant quality of energy somewhere in your body.

You're used to resisting this, used to running from it, but this time you're going to seek it out and immerse your attention in it. Notice that what you are feeling is the energy of the emotion of discomfort or fear of overwhelm that you always experience in your body but rarely notice.

Where is that energy most intense? Detect where you are experiencing it, and zoom in on it. You may find that it's somewhat generalized, or that it's in more than one place. Sense around to determine where the strongest energy is located. Don't let yourself get distracted; it may seem a little scary, but nothing there can hurt you.

Now that you've located that energy and zoomed in on it, allow your attention to penetrate right into the core of the most concentrated part of it. You may again find some resistance to going there, or it may feel hard to get in, which is another form of resistance. Again, this is normal. Allow yourself to continue to focus on the sensation you're feeling. If it helps, imagine a laser piercing the resistance, or imagine squeezing a lubricant into the area to allow your awareness to slip inside it.

Stay with it and simply observe the energy and allow it. If you notice there's resistance and fear of entering it or being within it, know that it's an illusion; what is there will not be hard to bear. Tears may momentarily swell as you move through a barrier of resistance; don't get caught up in tears, but recognize they may represent another layer of resistance, and continue to train your focus on the energy. Allow yourself to be curious about the energy that is there. Focus on the quality of the energy rather than the emotions or stories about the energy. Simply permit yourself to experience the energy rather than creating a story about it. Sense the energy. What is its quality? Is it hot, cold, moving, dark, colored, big, small, etc? What, if anything, is it doing? Is its quality changing in any way?

Let your awareness remain at the center of the energy. If the energy moves to another place, simply follow it, locate where it is most powerful or intense, and again drop your attention down into the very core of it. Continue to stay in this place, observing without judging or resisting.

You will probably find that the energy is dissipating or vaporizing, or that its quality is changing from something that is uncomfortable to something that feels more calm and peaceful. If there is any lingering energy, or it's less intense but still there, continue focusing the gaze of your awareness into the center of it. As it leaves, gather up what is left and continue until it has either lifted off or transformed into something soothing or feels like nothing at all.

In some cases, you may find that there is more than one layer of feeling there. If so, find the core of the energy of each feeling and feel down into it, until the energy is no longer uncomfortable.

Congratulations! You've just dissolved overwhelm! What you were avoiding turned out to be a hologram. It seemed like it had the power to overcome you, but that was only an illusion. By avoiding it, resisting it, or denying it, you build its power to stop you. Procrastination is the result. By maintaining your focus on it, though, you remove the sting you believe it might have. It's painless and simple. It hasn't killed you, and you actually now have the experience of knowing that you're capable of handling what appears to be uncomfortable or scary feelings. You can practice this and know that you can manage almost any feeling without it overwhelming you.

Mastering this ability allows you to quickly come out

of the grip of any emotion. Practicing this technique whenever you are about to procrastinate allows you to notice what it is that you have been avoiding experiencing and allow yourself to start experiencing it. You actually have a much greater capacity to handle seemingly unpleasant or distressing sensations (as well as powerfully positive ones) than you thought you did. That capacity has been there, but your pattern has not allowed you to experience it. You have just had a habit of keeping a lid on accessing that capacity.

There are over 2000 emails that have accumulated in Janet's in-box. It hadn't been so much of a problem in the past, she explains nervously, aware that other people use e-mail as a way to procrastinate, or are so distracted by it that they don't get other things done. She admits that she's overwhelmed by it. It started when she went away for a week, and came back to over 250 emails. She opened a few, but more kept coming in, and she couldn't keep up with it. As it mounted to over 1000, she felt inundated. That's when she started avoiding it. Now it had become a real problem—people were waiting for replies and had called her to see if something was wrong with her. She knew she had to take action, but facing it felt like locking herself in a room full of angry snakes. Dissolving Overwhelm would be a good place to start.

At first, Janet had a hard time finding any physical tension while contemplating her emails, and then she felt tension everywhere. Eventually, she found its center in her knees. It took a few minutes to find her way through it, but within fifteen minutes, there was no more tension. It had disappeared. What replaced it was an eagerness to get to work on reducing the number of e-mails in that inbox.

By the next morning Janet had reduced her inbox emails from 2000 to less than 300. While that was still quite a few, it was now much more manageable, and she knew that she would have no problem keeping things manageable.

If you're like most people who have dissolved overwhelm, you'll now notice that the task you were about to avoid no longer seems as onerous, difficult, scary, or boring. There is nothing blocking your progress. You've just dissolved the block. The block was only a sensation, a feeling, a form of energy you hadn't fully experienced until now.

Sometimes while you're doing this technique images may appear to you, or thoughts may occur to you. This may be useful information. Don't follow the images or thoughts down their rabbit hole, though, as this may distract you from the purpose of the exercise. This practice allows you to utilize more than just your mind, and allows your mind to temporarily be on reprieve while you notice what your senses may have to tell you. Additional benefits you may get while practicing this technique include receiving intuitive hits, noticing interesting or useful things you hadn't paid attention to

before, or having realizations pop into your awareness.

Some people find Dissolving Overwhelm hard to do on their own. Their minds take over and dart like a pinball from thought to thought, never penetrating enough to accomplish much, or they get so far with it, but without guidance and support they skip off the surface of the overwhelm. It this describes you, here are some suggestions: read the exercise slowly and clearly into a recorder, then listen back to it. Don't rush the process. Sometimes it's very quick, requiring only a couple of minutes, and sometimes it can take twenty or thirty minutes—allow enough time to get through it and be patient. There are guided Dissolving Overwhelm recordings available at **StopProcrastinatingNow.com** that you can purchase, including eight procrastination coaching sessions, some of which include this exercise.

Chapter 11
Tapping Into the Power of Inspiration

A number of years ago, when I first began my coaching business, much of my work focused on helping people get rid of their clutter and organize their lives. It didn't take long to realize that while being organized was what my clients and workshop participants really seemed to want, enough to overcome their embarrassment and let me into their cluttered, messy private spaces, their overwhelm and distaste for the process was a huge drag on their efforts. It was like they had a bulky, heavy obstacle in their way, and the attempts they'd made at getting organized where like pushing the obstacle down the road in front of them. It took a lot of energy and they couldn't do it for very long before they'd get worn out. I'd look for ways around the obstacle, and some of them would work, at least for a time. Sometimes they found the same obstacle, or a similar one, a little further down the road.

Eventually, I found some ways to clear the path entirely. One of them, Dissolving Overwhelm, was explained in the last chapter. That was like going straight into and through the obstacle, and finding that it wasn't real. Some people find Dissolving Overwhelm too "woo-woo." Even though it's the most effective and sustainable technique to address procrastination (and other distress, worry, and unhappiness), they haven't much interest in trying it or using it on a regular basis.

Desire vs. dread

But there's another excellent strategy that lifts and encourages them above the fray of their competing intentions in some way: inspiration. What I developed over time was a simple system to help them identify both the costs associated with delaying, and develop more enthusiasm for beginning. Even though there's nothing new about making lists of pros and cons, nobody I've ever met has ever made one about getting organized and accomplishing their desires. When applied this way a well-crafted list is a superb motivational technique.

Rita, a participant in an early workshop designed to introduce people to the way I might help them get organized (and to allow them to gauge their interest in a follow-up five-week course) arrived with trepidation. I always begin my workshops by asking what attracted each participant, and what each of them wanted to walk away with. Rita said that, honestly, even the thought of de-cluttering made her short of breath and turned her stomach into knots. While I expressed my concern that I didn't want her to have a heart attack or nervous breakdown in the class, and that she was free to leave at any time the discomfort level got too high, she stayed, and to my surprise she signed on for the five-week follow-up course, as well.

The course ran weekly for five weeks, for an hour each week. At the beginning of each week's hour, I'd ask how everyone had been progressing since we'd last met. We'd celebrate progress and trouble-shoot difficulty and inaction, before getting into the meat of that week's content. During the fourth week of the course Rita attended, she mentioned she was frustrated. When I asked her why, she replied, "Because I want to spend more time de-cluttering, but I have so many work and personal commitments that I can't find more time to organize things." I paused because I had to do a mental double-take. Wait a minute, wasn't this the woman who had physical symptoms at just the thought of getting organized? Hadn't she warned us that she was going to have difficulty following through? We were all impressed—and curious. I asked Rita what accounted for this wonderful internal realignment, and she said that it was focusing on how getting spaces clear and ordered would free her up for what she really wanted to pursue. The introductory class's initial focus on benefits and payoff of getting organized placed her attention squarely on how life would be post-clutter rather than the arduous process of getting there. Rita was drawn into the organizing process by the mental picture of a more relaxed and serene lifestyle, one in which she looked forward to having people come over and socialize instead of being ashamed of her apartment. She wanted to pursue new career goals and sensed that she would easily be able to handle any challenges and glitches that might arise because she was on top of her game, organized and ready for action.

Creating a vision

This is what I call a vision: a picture of what life will feel and look like when you have created the new habits that put you on the path to productivity and satisfaction. It's a powerful image that generates energy and enthusiasm. The image and sensation that you create will be different from anyone else's, and how it looks is specific to any particular situation. Its effect is to create a positive approach to the objective, one that you're pulled to like a magnet.

When I run classes and workshops I ask participants to create a list they will keep in front of them over the next few days. I request they take a blank sheet of paper and make a line from top to bottom in the middle of the sheet, so there are two columns: a column on the left and one on the right. At the top of the left side of the page I ask them to make a "frownie" face, with the word "Cost" under it, and on the top right side a "smiley" face with the word "Payoff" under it. It looks like this:

COST	PAYOFF

We then spend some time discussing and writing down all the ways procrastination is costing us with this specific task; this gets recorded in the "Cost" section.

The kinds of things that most frequently get listed include:

- Lost time
- Lost money
- Lost energy
- Loss of a sense of control
- Loss or lessening of confidence in your abilities overall
- Stress
- Lack of peace of mind
- Farther from a sense of freedom
- Aggravation
- Anxiety
- Dread
- Feeling of distraction
- Missed business opportunities
- Conflict in relationships

Of course, the list is endless, but these are the most commonly mentioned ways people are paying for procrastinating on getting and staying on top of their clutter and paperwork. The purpose of this part of the exercise is to establish a full awareness of the total "expense" to you at this point. Until you make the effort to complete this side of the page, there's usually a lack of awareness, not to mention a denial, of how much you're paying by putting off dealing with your piles of stuff and list of to-do's. This part of the exercise is helpful and motivational because you come face to face with the many ways and the full breadth of current and continued delay. At the end of the litany of costs we compile, I always ask, "Is everyone sufficiently depressed now?" This side of the exercise has a certain effect. For most people it isn't a comfortable sensation. Notice how low your sense of possibility is at this moment. It's not the most productive place to be, right? But it gives us a springboard for the rest of the exercise. It's where the right side of the page comes in.

The "Payoff" side is all about what you *do* want rather than what you *don't* want. What you list on this side is not "relief from" but what it will feel and look like once you get that "relief from." So, for instance, if a cost is distraction, the payoff might be the ability to focus with little or no effort. If you are experiencing stress as a cost, the payoff could be peace of mind, or a sense of calm, or the space for your creativity to blossom. If procrastination is costing you discord with your colleagues, spouse, kids, or friends, the payoff for creating a habit of following through may be more harmony, pleasure, and sense of safety in those relationships. This side of the page is for what you're running *to* rather than running *away from,* because there's a whole different feeling on this side. Now you're working with inspiration, the distinct impression of opportunities and of opening up, as opposed to a sense of distaste, unwelcome effort, trepidation, or feeling stuck or shut down.

Make your payoff side as juicy and appealing as you can. The more engaging and attractive it is, the higher the likelihood you'll take action toward it. Remember to phrase the entries on the right side of the page as qualities you'd really love to experience rather than "relief from" something yucky. Use the entries on the left (cost) side of the page as fuel for the right (payoff) side. If shame and guilt are costs, associated payoffs might be a sense of satisfaction and self-respect, or the feeling of feeling competent, capable, and virtuous.

Create your own page, and keep it in front of you for the next few days, moving it from place to place to keep it fresh and visible. Create it now and put it on your pillow so you see it before you go to bed tonight. When you see it on your pillow later, take it to where you have your morning coffee so you'll see it there in the morning. From there, you might put it on your briefcase or on top of the television remote. You're getting the idea, which is to keep it in front of your eyes so it doesn't become a part of the scenery that you start ignoring. You're more likely to take action on what you're repeatedly exposed to, especially if it inspires you. You're simply "creating an environment" conducive to following through.

Cliff, a teleclass series participant, had wanted to wall off part of his large bedroom to build a home office. This was a goal he'd admitted to in the first week of the series, one that he'd harbored for years. We set about designing a set of internal and external environments to support him in pursuing this goal. Little did I know at the time how effective this technique could be, but Cliff's example really brought it home for me. By the fourth week of a five-week series he reported being 90% complete building (by himself) this new home office, complete with a built-in desk and shelving. Moreover, his business, which had been stagnant, was beginning to pick up. While Cliff missed the last week of the series, I contacted him about two weeks later to follow up on his progress. Cliff wrote,

"I can't explain it, but I simply had to create a

"professional" place for myself and my office and my business. Before, I haphazardly set up a transient office and there was no solidity or substance to it. It was as if it could be moved or disassembled at any time. It was reflective of my life. Now I have an entire room that is an office. It has become a project that my wife, Tina, and I can work on together and build together. Last night, we framed in and hung a map we bought. It looks great. We just keep looking at what we did, have done, are doing, and we see a lot of possibility in other areas of our house and lives. It was as if we created a ledge (8x13) and on that ledge we built something very unique, solid, and us. We've lived in the same house ten years and never "owned" it. We kept saying we would sell it soon, so we never personalized it. Our office is now personalized. It was quite scary. Quite a large task. Most of the impetus came from your class. I feel so much... different... professional...competent in this environment. You would not believe how many people are calling me now with opportunities and possibilities. People I haven't heard from in years.

There is no coincidence. I am reminded of the movie: "If you build it they will come." My life is taking a whole new turn. Over the weekend, I emptied the "Basket" that had been collecting papers for over four years. I filed the necessary ones, and threw out the old. I felt so agitated doing this, but I did it. Now I have only one more item to go through. I feel excited and scared. Now what? Now I have to produce at a higher level.

The bar has been raised, and can I cut the grade? Of course I know I can.

Across the ceiling Tina has been painting select phrases. The one that I get to look at all day is from the Ovid: "Love and fortune befriend the bold."

Inspiration = rocket fuel

Cliff's experience tapping into a vein of inspiration isn't unusual. There's something synergistic about inspiration. Your actions seem almost effortless and your productivity level soars. At the same time, rather than feeling drained by the prodigious output, you feel energized and enthusiastic about continuing. Inspiration is like having a free supply of rocket fuel, whereas discipline and willpower is like having to walk up a mountain carrying a seventy-five pound backpack.

Happily, inspiration can be generated in a number of ways. The Cost/Payoff Exercise above is one way. It reconnects you with the core intention behind your goal, which usually lies beneath layers of misleading conditioning and hobbling beliefs. A majority of people in the developed world, particularly in the United States, are overweight and out of shape. A very common pair of "goals" related to that is to lose weight and get fit. The usual means of accomplishing that, at least that I've heard and seen countless times from clients, workshop participants, and survey respondents, is to go on some diet or another, and work out at a fitness center. These are the actions most frequently considered and chosen to achieve the goal, mostly based on cultural influence and ideas. Limiting yourself to those avenues is narrow, confining, and usually doesn't work. But the twin "goals" of weight loss and getting fit are only a means to an end, and they're only one set of means.

The core intentions behind losing weight and getting fit are more basic: to feel more self-confident and comfortable with your appearance, to feel healthy and capable of physical exertion, and to sustain and extend your life—these are the real objectives. We feel much more attracted to them than to "losing weight" and "getting fit." We're more likely to follow through on what feels appealing.

What are the core intentions behind your goals? Keep asking yourself, "Why do I want that?" until you get to something like, "So I can enjoy my life wholeheartedly, unhindered by shame, embarrassment, or self-loathing, pursue my dreams without delay, and use my gifts without doubting or second-guessing myself." What you mentioned just before this last desire is much closer to your core intention as it relates to the task you're dragging your feet about.

Let's try this with three of the most frequent procrastination task mentioned: paperwork, housework, and taxes. Why do you want to get these things done? "Because they're due," you say. Well, sure they're due—they're probably overdue by now. Finishing your paper work, cleaning your house, and submitting your tax return will get you what? "They'll get me back in the good graces of my teacher, my partner, my accountant, and the government," you think. "It'll keep me out of trouble and contribute to maintaining relationships that are stable and safe." How does that help you? "Well," you reply, "that's one less thing to worry about, so I can focus on things that feel more important to me. A clearer desk and cleaner space leads to a clearer mind." Why does that matter? "A clearer mind and a mood unclouded by looming deadlines and consequences will let me pursue other things that are more pleasurable or more interesting." What more interesting pleasurable things? "Watching a movie with my kids or taking a walk in the park."

Do you see how we're going from a "should" to a "want," how we're re-focusing on what you could have rather than what you don't want?

Let's ramp up the magnetism even more through the following techniques: identifying with your hero, recognizing your greatness, and leveraging your victories.

Identify with your hero

We all have people we look up to, those who serve as a model for us in some way. They might be parents, teachers, and mentors. They are also fictional characters, historical figures, and mythical superheroes. Different people identify with different values, and situations or circumstances provoke different needs, so any one person may have many heroes. We treasure our heroes because they elicit in us the very qualities they embody, and they inspire us to follow their example. We identify with them because they mirror the same traits in us; if they didn't, we wouldn't admire them, we'd be indifferent to them. Whenever we're faced with a choice to procrastinate or not, we can call on them to guide us, figuratively or literally. It's sort of along the lines of the question, "What would Jesus do?"

One of my clients, Linda, is battling with clutter. When I ask who she could use as a hero to model herself after, at first she mentions her aunt, who has the neatest and most organized home she ever saw. As we discuss it, though, it turns out that her aunt isn't a good hero for Linda. She takes being organized too far for Linda's taste—almost obsessively so, Linda feels. You never feel at ease sitting down or touching anything in her house. She really doesn't want to be as organized as her aunt, nor approach it the same way.

As she sifts through her mental file of friends, family, acquaintances, and others, her friend Becky comes to mind. Becky has kids, as Linda does, and a busy lifestyle, and she maintains a house that's neat, but comfortably so. Becky is organized about her kids' activities, the way she runs her household and fulfills the church and PTA roles she's taken on, and how she fits it all in along with her part time job at a retail store. Becky can find what she needs when she needs to, and she seems to get a lot done. She's a perfect inspirational hero for Linda when it comes to getting and staying organized. When Linda brings in the mail, instead of plopping it on the kitchen counter and leaving it there, she thinks of how Becky might deal with it and goes to the recycling bin, throwing out 75% of it before she opens a thing. She puts the bills in her new bill box, puts her husband's mail on the table for him to look at, and puts the invitation for a fundraising event in her new tickler file for two weeks before the RSVP date.

Linda also wants to get in shape, but since Becky is about forty pounds overweight and gets winded going up a flight of stairs, she isn't a hero for Linda in this regard.

Instead, Linda picks a former supermodel, whom she'd seen on an infomercial. This supermodel had been slender and shapely, but gained weight and got out of shape after she had a couple of children—the infomercial even showed "before" photos of her when she was out of shape, as well as "after" photos! That is a real inspiration for Linda, since the supermodels before photos looked about the same as the shape Linda is currently in. Now, when it's time to work out or when she looks in the refrigerator for a snack she imagines what the supermodel would do, and does that. She keeps a photo of the supermodel on the fridge as an additional reminder.

What procrastination situation are you facing, and whom can you call into action as a hero?

Recognize your greatness

We're always criticizing ourselves for the ways we think we don't measure up, but rarely do we recognize or embrace any of our more wonderful qualities. Have you seen the inspirational emails that circulate about a teacher who had kids write nice things about each of the other kids in their class and then compile the compliments for each child and give them to each of the kids? In this inspirational e-mail, you read about how some of those kids kept those lists in their wallets for decades, about how when they were down, remembering or re-reading the list lifted them up and got them going. There are other similar emails about people who said good things to someone else, someone in the depths of despair, and how it saved that person. You can use the same idea to inspire yourself.

Write down the qualities you have seen in yourself that you're proud of. If you have a hard time thinking of much, ask friends, family, and co-workers to tell you what they admire about you and what they see as your potential. You'll probably have some very pleasant surprises. When you pay attention to what's great about you, it gives you more energy and confidence. It inspires you to live up to that greatness.

Whenever you get down on yourself, when you're at a crossroads, about to choose between destructive procrastination as a way to avoid discomfort, fear, boredom, or dread, versus stepping into action, ask yourself what's great about you.

Leverage your victories

You know that old chestnut "success breeds success"? Well, it's true. When you experience a victory it expands your confidence, gives you a greater set of tools and strategies that you can count on, helps you more easily recognize good opportunities, and puts you in a positive, can-do mindset.

Part of my daily planning and gratitude practice, which I do early in the morning, is to list the victories I've had in the last day or so. It's a great way to start the day on an upbeat note and gives me zest and enthusiasm for today's challenges. It also sets me up for an expectation of success rather than failure in the day's tasks. I don't always get everything on my list completed, but I'm almost always content that I've accomplished the important things and spent the day in worthwhile endeavors.

When strategizing how to overcome inertia and foot-dragging, I often ask my clients to refer back to some prior victories they've had. These victories usually contain the seeds of inspiration for them in their current procrastination considerations.

Eileen is having difficulty setting aside time to study for a test she has to take every year to stay in compliance with laws in the financial industry. She loves people, and she loves helping them, so she's successful in her career, but every year she has to deal with this test. She resents it. It diverts her from what she enjoys doing and is good at. Unfortunately, her resentment and frustration aren't serving her, but are only increasing her desire to further put off studying. There's no question, she must take the test, and she must pass. She's had some close calls in the last few years, where she almost missed the test and almost failed, and she doesn't want that to happen again.

When I ask Eileen about similar experiences she's had, ones where there was something necessary but she didn't enjoy doing the thing, she thought for a while, then mentioned how she'd handled studying in college, especially those required courses like statistics. She remembered the strategies she'd used, like buddying and using rewards or consequences (more about these in the next chapter), and how well they worked for her. Recalling her victory over statistics also put her back in touch with what "juiced" her about working in the financial world, as well as the fire she had for making a difference.

Implementing similar strategies is certainly helping her follow through on studying, but remembering the details of her victories in college, by itself, is going far to make studying less of a struggle

.

Chapter 12
Giving Yourself an Extra Edge

This chapter covers a number of practical nuts-and-bolts strategies, the basis of which you're probably already familiar with, but I've given most of them a twist and tweak to make them more effective.

Before you try any of them, please heed this advice: do not fall into the trap of thinking you've failed if you attempt some of these strategies and they don't work, or don't work as well as you'd like them to. Enter this realm with an attitude of experimentation and play. As my clients and I do, investing in your own success means you'll always be trying new techniques, playing with new concepts, bending and twisting methods so they work for you. It's rare that one system, process, or trick will work forever, so accept that as a rule of thumb.

I want you to know, since it's reassuring, that there are actually a number of habits and practices that will become second nature, that after a period of weeks or months of applying yourself will not take effort or struggle. "Weeks or months?!" you say? Yes, for habits like staying fit, keeping to a budget, maintaining an organized and tidy space, getting paperwork done on time, it will take some time. You've engaged in less productive habits for decades—that's a pretty deep pattern rut, and it will take a little while to forge a new path that's worn enough to feel comfortable. That's normal. Would you prefer to continue the same old bad habits for decades more? Doesn't a few weeks or months seem like a breeze compared to years or decades?

As with most procrastination, the short-term reward is more immediately pleasing than delayed reward. Research has shown that people who cultivate the practices of perseverance and delaying gratification are more successful. The Elite Performer Study™, conducted between 1987 and 1996 and evaluating over 15,000 individuals in over 200 industries, showed that self-control and discipline are one of six necessary key traits that top performers share. A Gallup poll of over 80,000 successful managers found that they intentionally or intuitively hired people who exhibited discipline, personal accountability, and responsibility.

Just because you might not currently be a model of discipline and personal accountability doesn't mean you can't develop those habits—that's right, habits, patterns of behavior. If you think, "That's not my personality," think again, because putting things off is simply a learned pattern that you can change at will, made easier when the right elements are in place to support new more productive patterns.

Plan it, chunk it, schedule it!

My Procrastinator Profiler Quiz data shows that about 15% of the population are what I call "unplanned procrastinators," people who mean to get things done but haven't thought about the steps needed to get there.

Another 32% of quiz takers are "overwhelmed procrastinators" who get daunted before they can think things through enough to create a plan. That's close to half the over 2700 people who have taken the quiz. About 4% of quiz takers were "fabulous-at-following-through anticrastinators" or "almost anticrastinators, so the quiz wasn't taken by only procrastinators.

Over and over again, when I talk to clients and workshop participants about the things they're not getting done, they haven't looked closely enough at those tasks and projects to see the individual steps. Or they think they need to schedule three hours at a time (and who has that kind of time these days?), or they haven't committed a date and time to doing it—or all three.

Examining a project or task and breaking it down into its component parts has a few useful points. You understand the next steps you need to take, you can see the chronology of how the steps fit together so you can more accurately estimate the amount of time you need to complete them, and you're less intimidated because you've taken a big, bad goal and minced it up into more manageable bites.

Don't get caught up in needing to be at the last step, finishing. Instead, as you're working your way through, focus only on the next step in the process. Schedule an hour. If you don't have a full hour, then just schedule half an hour. Even twenty minutes will usually get you going. Scheduling more than that is too difficult and off-putting, so keeping it shorter leads to more success.

Next, use a calendar, diary, or scheduler. Pick a specific date and a specific time slot on that date. I can't tell you how many people don't get things done because it never makes it from their to-do list onto their schedules—but it's an awful lot! The action of putting it on your calendar not only provides more structure and accountability, it also increases your commitment to following through. It won't always work as a stand-alone strategy, but it's a huge help.

Over-schedule

The best-laid plans can be screwed up by a million little and big things. You're about to start getting your tax receipts together and your best friend calls because she's had a big fight with her teenage daughter and needs your advice. You're ready to begin sorting and purging the stacks of magazines and mail on the appointed day and time, but the plumber needs to reschedule at that time to fix the leak under your sink. You're all set to get to the gym—you even have your gym bag in the car, but your boss needs you to stay late to finish a report that's due at 8 a.m. tomorrow morning—he'd meant to tell you this morning but was in meetings all day offsite, and the cell phone service was poor there.

Since the unthought-of so frequently gets in the way of our intentions, we have to create a means for dealing with it: over-scheduling. This concept has produced good results for my clients.

Instead of scheduling a single forty-five minute chunk of time this week for purging your old files, for example, schedule three chunks of forty-five minutes. If one or even two of those self-appointments get hijacked, you've still got it covered. If you'd like to complete three half-hour workouts, try scheduling five or six.

A bonus of this technique is if you want to work on the task more than the single session, you certainly can, but you're not obligated to.

Be careful not to blow off every appointment except the last one because you know there's still another chance to finish—it backfires and makes over-scheduling a worthless tactic.

Buddy up

Personal story: Earlier this year I was beginning to really feel pudgy, out-of-shape, and stiff. It had been over a month and a half since I stopped working out while I was in the process of moving. I have to admit that since I've never been much of a fan of exercise just for exercise sake; it was kind of nice to have an excuse to be "lazy."

Over the last ten years or so, through steady, consistent application of the techniques I use with clients and write about in my books, e-zines, and articles, I've been successful at following through with working out three to four times per week. I have a few dozen videos I've collected over the years to pick from so I don't get bored including techniques such as Pilates, Yoga, step or floor aerobics, fitness ball, and more.

Five o'clock in the morning works for me (yes, I know that's breathtakingly early for many of you) because I'll never have a conflicting appointment or a phone call I have to make—there's less of an opportunity for excuses to get in the way. When the workout is done it's over for the day. I don't have to think about it again until the next morning, or talk myself out of it.

Even so, each day I've been tempted to stay in bed and continue sleeping. Some days I do succumb to that temptation. Until this past week, I'd slept in for the previous month and a half. For a while there wasn't any suitable workout space, and once I got access to the space I had no working VCR player. Now that I think about it, I didn't really need space or a VCR to work out but I didn't consider it that way. I just kept assuming I was only a day or two away from getting the VCR to work and resuming my workouts.

I used to be better at managing to work out four days each week. By earlier this year, it had dropped to three times, and occasionally only twice per week. So after this new move, I knew I had to design a better strategy. And I found one using a strategy that's worked in the past: a buddy.

I asked my neighbors if any of them would like to work out with me at 5:00 a.m., and I found one. Joan comes over at 5:00 a.m., and we're now working out five days a week, not just three or four. It feels great that the workouts are already resulting in more flexibility, and I'm already experiencing an improvement in my energy level. The simple addition of having a buddy arriving on my doorstep each morning expecting to engage in exercise is a huge motivator. There's no fudging, no falling back to sleep after the alarm goes off.

I've used buddies for other purposes, too, with great results. Currently, I'm working with two different colleagues on particular projects, and I'm making much better progress with them than if I was attempting those projects alone. One colleague and I speak on the telephone twice per week for about ten to fifteen minutes each call. We set goals pertinent to each of our respective projects or objectives, and we always check in on the next call to see whether each of us followed through. Sometimes we don't make much headway between calls, but that's okay because over the weeks and months we've worked together, our overall results have been really enhanced. Using a buddy can be invaluable in helping you realize long-term or sustained goals. It can be the difference between success and failure.

Here's how to make the buddy strategy work for you:

Find someone with similar goals—you'll be able to better support each other and be more aligned in your endeavors together. Choose goals and tasks that are a little outside your comfort zone, not so much that they're overwhelming and not so little that it's a no-brainer and isn't really pushing you forward. Write those goals down so you can refer back to them next time you talk or meet with your buddy.

Set a regular time to buddy. Whether you're taking vigorous walks, getting organized, writing a book, or building your business, making a habitual time each day or week is critical to follow-through over time. Haphazard buddying leads to haphazard results.

Hold each other accountable, but gently so. You're there to support each other in achieving your respective goals, not to badger or be judgmental. Often there are good reasons why you might not have done something you said you would. Do not assign blame to yourself or your buddy, but instead look for better ways to make sure you and your buddy follow through next time. You also don't want to give yourselves so much rope that you don't get any benefit out of the relationship. That won't do either of you much good.

Don't forget to celebrate your accomplishments! Most of us don't appreciate or acknowledge how far we've come. Having a buddy can give you a more objective perspective and someone to celebrate your success with. Contrary to popular opinion, patting yourself on the back doesn't need make you complacent. What it does do is develop confidence in your ability to achieve other goals in life.

A single daily action

This procrastination elimination technique can be applied toward broader intentions, and is pretty easy to use. Say you've been putting off starting an exercise program. Getting to the gym is only one of many ways to get exercise, and there are lots of interesting and varied ways to accomplish the goal.

Compose a list of single daily actions that get you closer to the goal. Working out at the gym is certainly one of them. Others could include a run in the park, biking with your kids, taking the stairs instead of the elevator or escalator at work, doing fifty sit-ups, push-ups and/or chin-ups before you step in the shower, playing a pick-up basketball game, dancing to the radio, following along with a television exercise show…you get the idea. If you pick at least one of these every day, you're making steady progress toward your goal. You have greater flexibility, more options, and you needn't get to the gym in order to feel on-track.

Truth or consequences

If you're like most people, your parents probably used reward and consequence strategies pretty regularly when you were a child. If you got your homework done before dinner you could go out and play with friends, or watch a favorite television program. If you didn't clean up your room, you didn't get to go to the mall or to your friend's sleepover.

There's a reason your folks used "carrots" (rewards) and "sticks" (consequences)…they worked! And they can work very well for you as an adult, too, in procrastination eradication. In combination with the principles used in previous chapters, utilizing these strategies makes an already effective method into an almost effortless one.

Incorporating a reward or consequence (or both, if your goal or task is important enough, or you've had difficulty in creating an inspiring environment) is simple and straightforward. You first need to identify what will make it worth your while to get or to avoid, as an added incentive. The sky's the limit here, and you can use your imagination to make this fun and innovative, and to keep yourself fresh.

If you're worried about keeping your own word, or believe this is just "playing a mind game" with yourself and think you're too smart for that, it's just your resistance speaking. Many of the most intelligent and psychologically savvy people make use of these kinds of approaches to successfully accomplish their objectives.

Harry, a client who owned a medical practice, had gotten out of the habit of physical exercise. Before he had kids and a busy practice, he'd really enjoyed going to the gym and working out. It didn't hurt that he felt more energetic and felt and looked fit, as well. But life had progressed, and he now found himself struggling to fit a regular workout into his schedule. I suggested that he could use a consequence strategy (a "stick") to help him follow through. First, he could make sure to schedule the workouts into his weekly calendar, and next, he could ask his receptionist to remind him early in the day when his workouts were scheduled, as well as ask her to "protect" those timeslots unless an emergency arose. Finally, he could offer to give his receptionist $20 every time he *didn't* get to the gym.

Harry thought about it for a moment, and rejected the last step. The money wouldn't motivate him, he said, but allowing the receptionist to come in half an hour later the next morning if he didn't get to the gym would. Fortunately, the receptionist was an honest person with integrity, and had Harry's best interests in mind! The plan worked quite nicely.

More accountability tactics

I've said it before, but it bears repeating: make it easier to follow through than not to. If you can find effective ways to incorporate this vital element into your procrastination annihilation plan, you're much more likely to be successful. Accountability tactics are a valuable and simple way to include this.

You may have used some accountability tactics already. If they haven't worked then they haven't been designed to be compelling enough. Getting more innovative and creative by improving on a few straightforward themes will give your efforts a turbo-boost.

Mindy knew that her just-past-deadline habit for submitting particular quarterly reports was hurting her chances for a promotion. She had tried a few tricks to be more prompt about starting and finishing the reports, but so far nothing had worked. She found compiling the data and creating the text a boring process, and she felt that there were other responsibilities that were more important and needed more attention. Her boss, the business unit president, disagreed, though. Those reports were requested by the executive leadership team, and it was clearly part of Mindy's role to create them. There was no wiggle room. Instead, we had Mindy utilize an accountability tactic: she composed a timetable of all the small and large tasks required to complete the report, and she and her boss scheduled a weekly meeting to gauge and measure her progress.

A mastermind group is another excellent way of getting assistance and accountability. Choose two or three other people and have a weekly teleconference or in-person meeting where each of you takes ten or fifteen minutes to review recent steps forward, troubleshoot difficulties, commit to actions, and celebrate progress.

Go public

Tell everyone you're doing this thing and it'll motivate you because you'll be too embarrassed not to. Get selective groups of people you feel will support you in achieving your objective, such as co-workers, people who attend the same house of worship as you, your neighbors, or your kids. A twist on this technique is posting your intention someplace, like on a community bulletin board, in an ad (or press release!) in the local paper, an online chat room, or even posters plastered on telephone poles around your neighborhood.

I recall a news story from a few years back about a man who was very overweight, and had a health crisis. His doctor told him he'd be dead within a year if he didn't lose a substantial amount of weight. That got his attention. He came up with an innovative plan. He was single and mostly ate in restaurants as he wasn't a good cook, and he knew he'd lose weight if he couldn't eat out, so he placed "Reward" notices in all the restaurants within a large radius of where he lived. The notice had his photograph and explained that any person spotting him in a restaurant would earn a reward of $1000. That's a plan that employs a few negative consequences, ones strong enough to stimulate him to carry out his intention.

Some concluding suggestions

Every year, at the top of the year, we find ourselves making all kinds of resolutions and hoping we have the self-discipline to follow through (for at least a few weeks!). A 2005 WomensWallStreet.com survey indicated that "lose weight" came in at the top of resolution lists with 24% of the vote, followed by "exercise more" with 20%. But resolutions #3 and #4 were an unexpected "manage my money better" and "be more organized," coming in neck-in-neck, each with 16 percent of women's votes. And rounding out the top five resolutions for 2006 with 11% was "improve my career."

These resolutions have a common denominator I call "The Yuck Factor." It's all stuff we feel we should do, we know it's good for us, and we really do want these things to come to pass, BUT...doing them involves getting past the parts of them that we find distasteful, uncomfortable, scary, or just plain HARD! Conflicting intentions abound.

We've evolved to the stage (especially in 21st century America) where we just about believe it's a birthright that we should be able to live our lives with absolutely minimal discomfort, struggle, and stress. And for the most part, that's a good thing (hey, it's a GREAT thing!). But we'd never get anything accomplished if we were always in that comfort zone; there would be no motivation or inclination to do much of anything. The fact is, we need some Yuck Factor in order to live an interesting, meaningful, and satisfying life.

You've heard it before...stress can be good for us (until it turns to distress), but have you thought about how that applies to the things you know you need to do but put off because there's some pinch, some tension that's generated because you're resisting the Yuck Factor?

There's just no way around the uneasiness and somewhat offensive nature of some of the stuff we need to deal with. No matter how rich or smart or healthy or beautiful we are, there will always be requirements and necessities that we'd really like NOT to do.

So, sometimes the only answer (much as I hate to parrot a much-maligned multinational) is "just do it." Really. Just put that clothespin on your nose, roll up your sleeves, put on the figurative (or literal!) rubber gloves (or parachute!), and jump in (or out!). Sometimes it really is only about taking some personal responsibility, accepting that there are just some things we can't avoid, and reconciling ourselves with that actuality. It becomes a lot easier to handle when we fully accept that it's just part of the package.

It helps to know that the benefits go far beyond just having "done it." Some of the things you'll gain: courage, persistence, wisdom, peace of mind, self-confidence, a sense of accomplishment, and can-do attitude, at the very least.

Be aware of how much energy you're using by pushing against having to do something that's unavoidable. Isn't that uncomfortable? Is there a constant low-grade tension and stress you're enduring because you've been putting off something necessary? Is there some strain at work or at home because of important things left undone? You can reduce and even eliminate it by remembering to dissolve overwhelm whenever you feel resistance dragging you down.

Distraction-free zone

Know that any time you start on a task or project that, if you let them, there will almost always be potential for interruptions. *Don't get distracted.* Reduce interference from telephone calls, visitors, or other tasks that are beckoning you. Don't put on the television or radio, don't go get a snack, and don't start working on a different (easier) task. Stick to the work at hand and move through it. If it's helpful, ask someone to call you at the beginning and end of a task you've scheduled, and remind you that you're doing that task and only that task.

You can check your e-mail after you finish—use it as a reward afterward but avoid it during your scheduled task time. Voicemail will wait for you—it won't be that long until you can check it. Before you begin tell your kids that you're not available for the next ____ minutes, and that they can interrupt you only in the case of an emergency—you might want to define what is and isn't an emergency. When you find yourself being led astray, practice dissolving overwhelm either alone or with the help of a friend to keep you focused.

Keep starting

There are lots of things to get done, and some of them have to be done over regularly, much to our distaste (exercising, flossing our teeth, staying on top of the mail and papers that come in, paying bills and reconciling bank statements, filing, preparing tax returns). There will be challenges, obstacles, and setbacks; accept that it's sometimes inevitable, treat the obstacle, challenge, or setback as another task to tackle, use the dissolving overwhelm exercise, and just keep starting.

Part IV

Procrastination Organization

Chapter 13
A Few Words About Managing Procrastination in Your Business and Your Organization

Procrastination in organizations, and more specifically amongst individuals within them, has only increased as pressures to perform intensify. Global competition, next day delivery expectations, unforgiving boards of directors, stock analysts and shareholders, along with fax machines, cellular telephones, and instant messaging have created a 24/7/365 business world. Everyone feels like they're operating at a breakneck pace, with one person doing the job that two or three had done only five or ten years ago. We're all dancing as fast as we can, trying, and sometimes succeeding, to keep up with the tempo. Most of us are stressed out much of the time, and some of us are frazzled and burned out all the time.

Over the last five years or so I've noticed that more and more people are self-diagnosing with Attention Deficit Disorder. I've been anecdotally coming to the conclusion that our culture cultivates attention deficit. This is visible in the way television and movies have cut their scenes down to fractions of a second. The proliferation of articles in a single daily newspaper, or books available at the bookstore (even the number of book categories), or the number of channels available on a typical cable or satellite television line-up, overburdens our circuits.

While I've been somewhat casually noting this, Ned Hallowell at the Center for Cognitive and Emotional Health in Sudbury, Massachusetts has been diagnosing and treating people with ADD for twenty-five years. He's noticed that people who may not have ADD might have what he calls Attention Deficit Trait (ADT), which is caused by brain overload and is now epidemic in organizations. ADT can easily undermine a gifted executive, and he notes that the people coming to him with ADT have mushroomed by a factor of ten within the past decade.

Procrastination is a very real result of ADT.

Procrastination at work

Why has your department not achieved its benchmarks? Why haven't your managers completed their annual employee evaluations yet? Why haven't you yet sought that line of credit or hired that business manager? Why hasn't your team produced the desired results on time? It all boils down to conflicting intentions and beliefs, which then produce overwhelm, resulting in delayed action, lowered output, and reduced success.

If you're an executive or manager, and your employees are procrastinating on particular projects, it could be that they don't know how to approach or execute those projects, and they're afraid to ask, for fear they'll look bad.

Rule #1—Do not nag or denigrate

You've had people put you down and pester you to get things done, haven't you? It doesn't motivate you in a positive way, doesn't build your morale, doesn't endear you to the person who did it to you, and doesn't make you want to excel for that person. It will have the same effect when you do it to others (or yourself). Because we have so much experience being nagged and belittled it's become part of the way we interact with others in return. It's almost automatic, and it isn't productive.

Don't make a quick assumption that an employee or colleague is lazy or incompetent because they are dawdling on a project or report. There could be any number of other, more pertinent reasons. Instead of assuming...ask! Find out what is in the way of accomplishing the assignment using a non-judgmental line of questioning and tone. Ask the person to repeat the specifics of the purpose of the assignment, the materials needed, the processes to be followed, the interim and final deadlines, the expected outcomes of the assignment, the level of quality expected as well as how that quality is to be measured, to ensure a clear mutual understanding and uncover any mistaken impressions or directions.

Then create an agreement about consequences for not completing the assignment on time and to the standards specified. It's important to set realistic consequences, and even more important to follow through on enforcing them.

Communicate priorities

Be clear as to the priority levels for the position's various tasks, responsibilities, and projects. A common complaint about managers and executives is that everything is (equally) important. That produces a constant state of anxiety and doubt in the people who report to you. They are continuously worried about whether they're doing the right thing at any moment and what is going to come back and bite them, which in turn reduces optimal effectiveness, excellent quality work, and stellar productivity.

Any position has three essential processes or roles. There may be a dozen ancillary responsibilities, but they are not as important as the top three. Do you and does your employee know which is which?

Remember that few people were taught time management or organizational skills in school. Some lucky people are naturally good at it and others have sought some kind of course or program during their careers, but most people could use training and coaching in these areas to help them reach, and then exceed, the expectations of their positions. While this kind of training may seem not to have a direct-line reflection on the business's bottom line as sales and materials costs might, they do directly affect something that most businesses don't measure: employee morale and productivity. That costs more than you might think.

A 2006 study by the employee research firm ISR using survey data gathered from over 664,000 employees during a twelve-month period revealed that operating income improved by over 19% in companies with high levels of employee engagement, compared with a decrease in operating income of close to 33% in companies with low employee engagement. Companies with highly engaged employees saw earnings per share rise by 27.8%, but companies with low levels of employee engagement saw their earnings per share drop by 11.2%. Those are pretty significant findings.

As global competition continues to heat up it's unrealistic to expect that businesses will be able to relax their expectations for employee performance, and since we've learned a lot about how stress and burnout affect morale and profits we have to get creative and embrace a new paradigm to increase productivity and efficiency. Our businesses depend on it.

View ISR at
www.isrinsight.com/pdf/media/2006engagementbriefing.pdf

Recipe for Stopping the Cycle of Doing It at the Last Second

Here is a recipe that might prompt you to attend to things before they become problematic.

Ingredients:
- Your Dreaded Task
- Two sheets of Legal Paper
- One Pen
- One heaping cup of Consideration
- One large dollop of Honest

- Two level helpings of Memory
- One full pinch of Anticipation
- One Obvious and Conveniently Located Calendar

Directions:

Step 1. Using one sheet of Legal Paper and the pen, mix the heaping cup of Consideration to Your Dreaded Task, which will greatly reduce the opportunity for the yeast of overwhelm to make the mixture rise too fast. List the benefits of having it behind you and the ramifications of putting it off.

Step 2. Add the dollop of Honesty to the mix, including how it will affect your personal or work life, your health, your family, your co-workers, your finances, and your future.

Step 3. Fold in the two level helpings of Memory relating to how wonderful you felt when you accomplished something on time, and how awful it was when you delayed ruinously.

Step 4. Slowly stir in the full pinch of Anticipation, to alert you to whether you really want to live with the energy drain of an unattended task constantly nagging at you and distracting you from your best efforts.

Step 5. Let the mixture marinate for fifteen minutes, to bring out the flavors of timely action, and to soften the bitter taste of having to do the dreaded activity now.

Step 6. Using the second sheet of legal paper, design a plan of action and list of tasks, complete with artificial interim deadlines to assure on-time completion.

Step 7. Transfer contents of the second sheet of paper to the Obvious and Conveniently Located Calendar on appropriate dates, and bake until golden.

Part V

The Procrastination Diary

This diary was started as a technique to assist me in following through with writing *Productive Procrastination*. To get words flowing I'd write in the diary for a few minutes, then switch to writing the content of the book. It worked. I didn't use the diary technique every single time I had an appointment scheduled in my calendar to write, only when I had trouble making myself do so.

What follows are the trials and travails I experienced while attempting to accomplish a goal that was a continual procrastination invitation.

June 17—8:41 a.m.

It's already 8:41 a.m., more than ten minutes later than I'd scheduled to start writing. As the computer alarm rang, I was busy entering some credit card transactions I'd been meaning to process for the last week or so. I was now getting to it, but the alarm was telling me it was time to do something else important.

The few minutes I thought it would take me to process those credit card transactions were greatly enlarged by some circuitous activities. Thinking about it, it's really funny!

Earlier this morning, as I was entering one client's information, I realized that I didn't have her credit card information readily available, so I walked to my sunroom, where I keep my client files, to retrieve the information. As I bent over to open the cabinet where the files are kept, a citronella geranium on top of the cabinet caught me by the hair. This same overgrown plant had annoyed me similarly in the last two days, and now it had my attention.

Completely forgetting, for the moment, the reason for

my journey to the sunroom, I grabbed the scissors from the kitchen and started pruning then cleaning the dead leaves off the plant. Citronella geranium cuttings root well and I've established a few pots of them from cuttings from an original plant I'd gotten years ago. I couldn't let the pruned ends go to waste, now could I? Getting out the rooting hormone, I began making some cuttings, dipping them in hormone, and slipping them in holes made in the soil using a pencil.

Did you notice that I mentioned that I'd established a few pots of the same plant? Yes, they were all in the same room, and they all needed pruning, cleaning, and to have cuttings put in to fill out the pot.

Approximately forty minutes later I scooped up all the left over compostable material and dust-busted the floor. Now that I'd completed it, I put away the scissors and rooting hormone, and noticed the insurance claim form that I hadn't yet completed sitting on the kitchen table.

I'd been brainless enough to put some jewelry in my luggage on a return flight home from a long business conference, and all of the good stuff had been stolen. My homeowners insurance wanted me to file a claim with the airline first. While the airline's policy doesn't cover jewelry, my homeowners carrier wanted the denial of the claim from them (they don't make it easy, do they?). I had gathered some receipts and other paperwork the airline required and now had to copy it all and complete the claim form. It had been sitting there for four or five days by this point.

Divided between whether I should spend time on this now or get back into my office, I decided it would only take a minute to copy the documents (yeah, right), and went downstairs where the copier was. Ten minutes later, I returned and created a pile of the originals and copies, not yet filling in the claim form. That would have to wait. ("Until when?" I thought.)

Making my way back to the office, my computer monitor reminded me that I had been in the midst of entering a credit card transaction….oh! Right! Back to the sunroom for the file! Does this sound familiar?

It was just a minute or two later, when I was entering the information, that the alarm dinged to remind me I'd scheduled time to continue writing this book on procrastination. It took me ten more minutes to complete that transaction and one other, before I got to writing.

None of these tasks were crucial or had a definite deadline, so I allowed myself to be pulled by these activities, rather than not allowing myself to be diverted by them.

My life is chock full of details, and many of them can slip through the cracks or get lost in the shuffle if I'm not careful. Depending on how many responsibilities and obligations I have at the moment, the number of daily, weekly, monthly, quarterly, and yearly details varies, but almost always seems immense. While I use a variety of methods to help me get everything done, in the past it would feel overwhelming. I'd turn to television, food, computer solitaire, telephone conversations with friends, browsing through catalogs, and other activities to avoid experiencing that overwhelm.

I've learned, though, that I can and do use systems, structures, and processes to help me get things done and follow through on what's important, and not to sweat the rest. I learned four things.

First, I'd be more likely to follow through on something if there was some ramification that was worse than avoiding the task.

Second, the overwhelm I assumed I was experiencing was really *fear of or resistance to* experiencing overwhelm. In essence, I was under the illusion that I wouldn't be able to handle everything, that I'd somehow be overcome or destroyed when it seemed there were more details than I could cope with by the time they were due. I hadn't been aware of any of this, of course. It was just a default response that I'd developed through being raised, through training, socialization, education, and all the subtle manipulations we are all exposed to as we grow from newborn to adult. Babies don't have the brain hardware to process big feelings and emotions, and overwhelm is awful. Watching a child become overwhelmed by feelings, I can see how it seems to them that it's the end of the world. Even though the spindle cells, the brain apparatus that allows us to process complex emotions, grows as we do, we're still operating on that early conditioning to avoid overwhelm. We don't understand that our ability to process those feelings and get beyond them exists, and is simple and painless to use.

The third thing I'd learned was to be attentive to the negative thoughts about what the delay meant about who I was. Those thoughts said I was somehow incapable, not whole, had something essential missing, was bad or less-than or unworthy. More overwhelm! I appreciated that these were more training messages from the past, and I couldn't deny their presence (they'd only get more persistent), but I didn't have to let them control me.

The third led to the fourth realization: I was okay whether or not everything got done, on time or late. I understood that I was doing the best I could, and that while there was probably more I could do, judging and scolding myself for not measuring up wasn't helping me get things done *or* feel good about myself. Acknowledging all that I was doing (and doing right) was a step in a better direction. Added to that was an approach toward what wasn't yet done that involved one of imagination, experimentation, and openness that was so very different (and so much more effective) than the blame and punishment approach I'd been using in the past. This diary is an example.

June 18—9:07a.m.

It's 9:07, seven minutes after my scheduled time. Somehow, I'd gotten it into my head that I had a telephone appointment with a colleague at this time, but I'm mistaken. Instead, I've got writing scheduled. So much for having looked at my calendar a couple of hours ago and thinking I knew my schedule for the day.

Since just after 8:00 a.m. I've been on the phone on a monthly call with another colleague. She loves to talk and we were discussing moving strategies, but she'd kept going after 9:00 a.m. rolled around, and I finally stopped her at 9:03. By the time we got off the phone it was a minute or two later.

Then I called what I thought was 9:00 a.m. appointment, and while it was ringing I looked at my schedule and realized I was mistaken. Covering my blunder by confirming we were on for later today, I hung up feeling just slightly out of kilter. Perhaps my previous conversation about moving, and all that would entail (as well as how soon it would be), had gotten my brain a little scrambled.

I could scold myself but I won't. My mix-up is understandable, considering all that I've got going on.

Writing is on my schedule for this hour but another priority is nagging at me. I've got to schedule some classes that I'll be giving next month, and the deadline for submitting them is today. I'd scheduled it for yesterday from 4:00-5:00 p.m., but that was when the builder called. We still haven't broken ground for the house I'm building 1000 miles away in Florida. For the past month and a half, we've been negotiating the contract. We're getting closer, but I have to be out of this house on September 1st. While I'll be moving from here to our summerhouse in New York state's Catskills, I don't want to have to spend the whole winter there. In my desire to continue to move this very slowly rolling ball, I took the builder's call. By the time we ended, the hour was over. And I'd done nothing to schedule these classes.

Today's schedule is pretty full, leaving little time to get this done. Looking at it again just now, I see I have some time this afternoon, but hate the idea of leaving it until then as there might be urgencies that come up at that time that prevent me from working on it. The office is quiet right now, and it's a good time to deal with it.

So I will.

If I'm done before the hour ends, I'll come back to writing.

June 21—9:15 a.m.

A call with one of my clients went late and extended about twelve minutes into my writing time. That's a good indicator that I need to leave more time between coaching calls and writing blocks, and that I need to be better about ending sooner with clients even when I don't have a hard stop scheduled. Note to self: review scheduled times with this in mind.

Just as I ended with the client, Gracie came in the room, looking for attention and play. How could I resist that adorable puppy face, not to mention her persistent vigorous nudging of my elbow and arm? For two minutes we played, and I could see it wasn't going to be enough, so I got out one of the new toys she received at her birthday party yesterday (eight people, seven dogs, six gifts), and that occupied her, allowing me to get to this about fifteen minutes past the scheduled time.

I never did get back to writing last Friday. It took several hours of work to complete the task, and it did get done by deadline, but took quite a bit longer than expected. It was a good thing I'd considered that it might, and had left some time to complete it before the target date. It certainly felt good to not only have it done, but to have done it completely and well, and on time.

As I've been writing this, it's been occurring to me that I could simply have fun with this diary ad infinitum (ad nauseum?), and never get back to the body of the book. It may also turn out that I get bored or resistant to doing this. Then where would I be? Aware that these thoughts are coming from a mindset of doubt, and amused that my focus isn't on the enjoyment I'm experiencing right now (instead giving attention to something that might or might not happen some time in the future), I relax into the pleasure of continuing this diary.

Excuse me for a minute, while I'm momentarily distracted by Gracie bringing my sneaker into the room. Have to retrieve it from the retriever before she licks it to death or chews the shoelace.

Okay, sneakers are put away, and thanks to Gracie for the reminder. Apparently, the new toy wasn't particularly compelling (despite the promising marketing copy on the label!). I took the break to put some coffee on, too, though it distracted me only for a moment from this task.

Ah...crucial moment. I've reached a brain freeze on this diary. Where do I go from here? Shouldn't I train my attention on the body of the book? I ask myself "So, what do I want more, to have this book finished and behind me, or to play with this?" It turns out that the choice isn't that simple—competing desires and beliefs are warring with each other.

The more I enjoy writing the book the better it will be, I believe. If my goal is to have it written so I can move on to other things rather than enjoy the process and produce a worthwhile resource for others, my attitude about it is that it's something to be gotten out of the way. The end product may suffer because it's then seen as a task to be quickly finished, with the objective being almost completely about what opportunities the published book might bring rather than what I might learn and be able to incorporate by the doing of it.

A computer reminder just dinged. I've got fifteen minutes until I'm scheduled to work on updating my website, a task that I've put aside for the last couple of weeks, and one I've had on my to-do list. Silly me, how could it not have occurred to me that I should simply schedule it on my calendar. This is even more remarkable to me since scheduling priorities is what I strongly recommend as one of the first strategies for accomplishing things! How could it have taken me a week to realize this was the difference between it sitting on the to-do list and getting it done?

The brain babble is saying "Stupid girl! What were you thinking?" but I'm choosing to laugh at it instead, knowing that the lighter approach allows me to continue easily instead of getting upset and frustrated with myself, growing more delay-inducing self-doubt.

June 22—8:39 a.m.

It's amazing how correspondence, which had been just about the only method of communicating over distance for the past number of centuries, and then took a real nosedive with the advent of the telephone, is now such a significant time vampire.

While these days we use immediately delivered e-mail and IM rather than handwritten letters conveyed by messenger, it's ironic that while many of its finer arts and aspects have been lost, for many people writing to others is much more of a daily routine (and stressor!) than it's ever been. Ten or eight, maybe even five years ago, we indiscriminately subscribed to all kinds of e-zines, looking for at least a couple of emails in our boxes each day. Now we're deleting e-mail with abandon, whenever we can!

Every corporate audience I've presented to complains about e-mail. If it's not spam, their complaint revolves around all the company memos, the cc's that they're included in because of projects they're involved in, the c.y.a. ("cover your 'butt'") emails that their colleagues/bosses/employees send, in addition to the substantial amount of posts they must respond to within their normal responsibilities.

You guessed it. I write this having been nine minutes late for today's writing schedule, due specifically to being in the midst of (and wanting to complete and get sent promptly to its recipients) an important e-mail post. That post took me about twelve minutes to compose, adjust, proofread, tweak, and send. That's about seven minutes longer than I guessed it would take.

While I've developed techniques for dealing with e-mail efficiently, sometimes those techniques don't result in as streamlined and rapid a process as I'd like. Spam filters, using auto-preview to view the first couple of lines of the e-mail, deleting all leftover spam or posts I don't want to read before I open anything else, and using folders to sort mail into help substantially.

If you're anything like me, you use the same techniques but still find yourself looking at that inbox and, at least a couple of times each week, wondering how you're going to get through all of it in a timely way and still get your other work done.

Culturally, e-mail has become at least equal to if not more urgent a message format than voicemail. Depending upon whether it's work related, the relationship between the sender and receiver, and the subject, one is generally expected to reply sometime within twenty-four hours, and sometimes in as little as thirty minutes. That's a lot of pressure, especially when you're getting 150 to 200 messages each day!

Certainly, not everyone uses e-mail. But in my discussions with clients, workshop participants, colleagues, friends, and family, those who do use e-mail are finding themselves spending increasing amounts of time on it, and we're all searching for ways to minimize the amount of posts and our time dealing with it.

When I find myself looking at an e-mail inbox with over 200 unread messages, there's a sense of things being out of control, then one of my feeling incapable of handling it, then of not wanting to! A sense of calm and confidence returns as I think back on my experience with it: nothing really bad has ever happened because I wasn't able to read and/or answer all my emails every day. I *can* and do manage it, necessary communiqués get read and replied to, and my business, my career, and my life are all fine even when I've gone away and not been able to see a single e-mail for days (and come back to well over 1000 emails). I *can* handle it, and I do. If not now, then a little later.

In an article entitled "What Makes An Effective Executive" by Peter Drucker in a recent issue of Harvard Business Review (June 2004), Mr. Drucker reports that the first thing that all effective execs do is answer the question, "What needs to be done?" with "What is right for the enterprise?" (having "stated objectives of the organization or initiative" in mind). Then they set and stick to the priorities based on that answer, postponing everything else (even if it is important!). More pointedly, after those tasks are handled, rather than go to the next items on the priority list, the question "What needs to be done?" is asked again, and this results in a new set of priorities. While it seems counter-intuitive that this would have excellent results, because of constantly shifting prioritization, it works because "what needs to be done" is always asked in the moment and is based on a longer-term objective than just the moment's seemingly urgent need.

Interestingly, there was another article in the same issue of Harvard Business Review: "Chronic Time Abuse" by Steven Berglas. He also concludes that managing time is essentially useless for those people who abuse time, because that time abuse is a symptom rather than the problem itself.

June 23—9:01 a.m.

Only one minute late today! It's a miracle!

Just kidding. It was an effort, though, to pull myself away from the task I'd been working on just prior to this. Even though it wasn't particularly interesting or exciting, I didn't want to stop working on updating the New Leaf Systems website, mostly because I wanted it to be done rather than left hanging. I didn't want to have to return to it at a later time (excuse me while I schedule that into my calendar, though).

I'm amused at this situation, since only about forty-five minutes beforehand, I found myself resisting working on the website altogether. And now it's hard to *not* do so! As we say in New York, "Whatzup with that?"

Checking in with myself about the resistance, there are a half dozen items on this morning's to-do list, and all of these things are bouncing around in my head. I want to complete them so I can concentrate more fully on other tasks. Knowing that these other things are waiting might distract me from the tasks scheduled on my calendar. Naturally, I want to operate with a clear head.

What to do…? Since there will always be more to do than I can fit into a day (I've long ago accepted this as truth), I make a note as to when I can fit some of those tasks into my day. I look again at the tasks that aren't already scheduled, just listed as tasks to take care of:

- Write a thank you note to my aunt for my birthday gift (it's been over a week)
- Write thank you notes to two authors for participating in conference calls last night

- Study some new resources I purchased
- Complete a client payment credit card transaction
- Call the property developer where I'm building my house regarding some questions I have

As I examine this list, it becomes apparent that there is nothing that absolutely must get done today. There will be more items tomorrow, and I'd absolutely prefer to get these done today, but while some are important, none are very urgent, and if none of them got done, my life would not fall apart. They are all preferences rather than necessities. While this doesn't give me the excuse to blow them all off, it relaxes me to know that I have the option to get them done, without the pressure of needing to.

June 28—9:00 a.m.

It *did* take a bit of discipline to heel myself to writing this morning, what with an inbox full of breathlessly awaiting emails to answer, doggy health-care concerns to perform (didn't you play veterinarian when you were little?), the don't-leave-home-without-it application of cosmetics, and the already-open web pages that begged to be read. But here I am, less than a quarter of an hour past schedule.

While there are so many things to relate, weighing heavily on my conscience is the fact that I completely and utterly missed last Thursday's and Friday's appointments with myself, and I simply have to come clean about it. I though I could just let it go and not address it at all, as if my dear readers wouldn't have duly noted it. Knowing at least *one* person would, I want to address this so it doesn't infringe on my clear-headedness, or my integrity.

Just before the Thursday's scheduled time slot, I got a

call from a colleague I was to meet with later in the day, requesting I bring my calendar. Since I was also bringing another document with me that resided in my e-mail program, I figured it best to back up my documents and e-mail folders onto my laptop to bring it with me. Very conveniently (though it did feel inconvenient at the time, as I was truly looking forward to writing), this required the full attention of both my desktop PC and my laptop, preventing me from utilizing either. I briefly flirted with the (very novel) idea of actually handwriting the diary, which quickly got dashed on the rocks of "it will take too much time to type it in afterward."

It was, of course, a complete no-brainer to fill the hour with all sorts of useful activities, all except for writing. But, happily, I felt I had made a choice about this, and was alright with it. As writing seems to be progressing well, I felt I could afford this day off.

Then came Friday, a day on which I felt unusually tired, and got something of a late start. As I was visiting the same colleague for the entire day, my attentions were focused on grooming and dressing, and the preparation for, and enjoyment of, working with him on the projects we were accomplishing. I toyed with the idea of appearing at his office later (which could have been acceptable as we hadn't set a definite time), staying at my desk long enough to write *something, anything.* On this day, however, it was not to be; I felt energized by the prospects of the day, as well as a bit pressured by the items on my to-do list to get in gear and get out the door. Hanging out writing didn't feel like a viable option at the time, and the choice I made was to get going rather than write. It was a choice, though.

Parts of me were resisting this ("Two days in a row!

You slacker!"), but I rested in the faith that I'd be back here this morning, prodigiously typing away; and look at that...I am!

June 29—9:18 a.m.

So many sirens sang their beckoning call this morning, leading me away from writing: the website on moving scams I'd opened earlier this morning, but hadn't yet read, revamping more text on my website, bringing a small paper calendar I keep as a diary up to date with all the appointments from my computer (so I can refer to it in later years without needing the same software, which will likely be obsolete by then), making a couple of telephone calls to clear up some details. None of these things, however, was what actually delayed this morning's writing. No, it was something else. Just prior to my morning shower I was seized by the sudden need to thoroughly scrub down the entire bathroom countertop.

Because a client had needed to reschedule, my schedule is more flexible this morning, and I could afford to spend time doing that, knowing I'd be able to shift things around a bit. It gives me a little thrill to rebel against my schedule, but within bounds. Silly, isn't it? It's like a creative little game I can play to see how unorthodox I can be and still get everything done.

A mnemonic device I've used before and have recently been using again has been delighting and amusing me.

The night before last, while lying in bed, I abruptly remembered that a number of library books I had taken out would be due soon. Luckily, a wonderful online system allows users to not only reserve books online from the entire library system database, but also to renew those that they have out, provided they're not already late. The truth is, I often forget to take advantage of this brilliant feature until the day they're due. However, that evening as my conscious brain was preparing for its nightly shutdown, it occurred to me to use it.

Getting out of bed at that time, however, wasn't something I wanted to do. How could I remember to renew them without having to leave the cozy confines of my comforter? Ah yes, the handy-dandy "tie it" memory trick might work nicely.

I thought of an activity that I would definitely, without a doubt, be doing the next morning. When my computer boots up, MSN Messenger displays two windows; I normally minimize or shut both once the boot is completed. I made a note in my mind, however, to tie the library renewal to the minimizing or shutting of those Messenger windows.

Now, this only works if you spend a few seconds concentrating on the activities you're tying together. I focused intently on seeing those windows displayed on my monitor—and then promptly fell asleep.

The next morning, sure enough, those Messenger windows were there, and prompted me to remember…what?

The night before I'd aimed the bulk of my concentration on remembering the windows, but very little on the task I was tying to shutting them! I was simply blank about what I was supposed to do. Fortunately, a few hours later, I remembered, and renewed the books.

Keeping this lesson in mind, I tied a new task to this morning's boot up: e-mail an associate to set up a meeting. This time, I put my attention on her name. It worked like a charm.

I have many stories like this, but my favorite, which I've told to many an audience, follows. It is slightly off-color, so you may want to skip down to the next day's entry if you find offensive anything even hinting of animal waste.

My dogs always get at least one walk around the block each day, and have for years. (They also get walks elsewhere, but now I'm getting off track.) One day, a few years ago, during one such walk I had cleaned up after my dog. Our walk had just begun, though, and I didn't want to have to carry the bag for another mile, so I put it down in a temporary spot in front of a neighbor's house, meaning to pick it up on the way back through.

Of course, I didn't remember it. That is, until later on that day when I opened my mailbox and found that someone had placed the reeking bag inside. I had to have a better plan.

A few days later, when I had another bag that I didn't want to walk a mile with, I did it again, left the bag and forgot to pick it up on my way through—and didn't have time at the moment to retrieve it. So I made a mental note to tie picking up the bag to something I'd definitely be doing in just a few minutes: getting the mail from my box when my returned from the important/urgent errand I was about to run.

In my mind's eye, I pictured myself opening the hinged door of the mailbox with picking up the bag. Keeping that in mind for a few seconds, I then finished my walk and went on my errand without a second thought.

As I returned, I stopped at the mailbox, oblivious to

the tie I'd made...until my finger touched that hinged door. Like a cartoon bubble popping up, the thought to pick up the left-behind-bag burst into my awareness. With the pick up successfully then made, I only hoped that I wouldn't find someone else's doggy waste in my mailbox in future (and I haven't!).

June 30—10:02 a.m.

Honestly, I'm feeling a little annoyed at the moment. Having just gotten off the telephone with the attorney who is helping me with my building contract (and if you've ever worked with builders it's likely you'll remember the challenges that come with that territory), I'm not in quite as positive a place as I'd prefer to be. Combined with the push to get things accomplished before leaving on a holiday break tomorrow morning, my desire to complete an important e-mail that I'd been working on prior to the call with the attorney created some friction when I noticed that it was just past time to write.

But write I do! I was tempted to let the urgencies of the moment dictate my activities. Even as I type this, my mind wanders a bit to "What do I need to be packing for this trip tomorrow?" At the same time, though, I connect with the internal knowledge that I will accomplish what needs to be completed (to the degree it needs to be done, and that this will be enough); that allowing the many to-do's swirling in my head to overwhelm me only takes me further from functioning optimally.

In the end, what really matters to me? I want to live fully, which includes actively and courageously putting myself out into the world to accomplish well those things that are meaningful to me. For me, that means that I get to enjoy the wonder, pleasure, delight, sacredness, and oneness that I experience with animals, nature, myself, and others. The route to happiness and fulfillment, for me, is the recognition of and participation in these things, and the self-compassion which allows us to be easy with ourselves and others, and can be reached through this very same connection. I'm tickled when I can share that with others—without forcing it on them.

My aim is to be a shining and visible example of someone who lives relatively lightly on the earth while still living a life that can be considered successful, happy, meaningful, and admirable by many people. Others would want to follow that example because of what it might offer them, because they're attracted to it through sensing the ease of it and the lack of struggle, problems, emptiness that haunt many "successful" people.

The end result is not fame-seeking, but to help contribute to something larger than my own happiness, because that happiness will be increased when others can accept and treasure the intelligence, sentience, and value of other life forms; to want to respect and protect them, coming from a place of not only connection to those things, but to themselves and others, making the world, or at least some of it, less hell and more heaven.

Well, that was a rant! Time for some coffee.

July 6—9:00 a.m.

The words are not coming. Staring at my fingers, or off into space, my mind is seeking other points of interest and is resisting focus on writing. Even these previous two sentences have been an effort as, rather than simply pour out thoughts, my mind's inclination is to edit as I write rather than get it all down and adjust it later. While not quite perfectionism, I recognize it as a typical block for procrastinators, particularly for people needing to write something. If it's not a good product, why bother? Why spend time on something I'll have to spend more time fixing later? I want anything I do to be stellar, or at least as close to perfect as I can make it. These thoughts, of course, are the language of the perfectionist. Behind them is a strong need to not fail, to be above criticism.

It's an illusion, though. No matter what we do, we will sometimes fail, unless we rarely do anything at all. And no matter how brilliantly we perform, someone somewhere will be able to find fault in some way. To let this affect daily performance is just plain silly, and more common than we ever imagine.

There are many authors who have written wonderful books that have turned out to be commercial flops, only to have other books they consider to be mediocre evidence of their talents become best-sellers. There's no guarantee. I could allow all this information to stop me, but that's not the choice I'm going to make.

I allow myself to pay attention to the vague but insistent desire to avoid, or to resist. I listen more closely. "I have nothing to say!" it bleats. "There's nothing of value inside of me to translate through my fingers to this screen. Who am I to think I can write something that people will really find useful? Will I ever really finish this book, and will anything ever really come of it? Is this an exercise in futility, in self-indulgence?"

Once I acknowledge what these thoughts are and how they're blocking me, I can let go of them. Unacknowledged, they sit and fester and twist my energy into something useless or, worse, destructive.

July 12—9:15 a.m.

It's 9:15 a.m. and somehow the computer reminder (and palm device) either didn't ring, or my awareness ignored it. From the looks of it, it's the latter.

Having been away for some time on vacation and presenting at a conference, I've got hundreds of emails to read. Taking a few minutes after a client call, which ended at 8:54 a.m., to weed out spam and junk e-mail, by the time I'd whittled the inbox from 410 to 57, it was suddenly 9:08. How had I missed not one, but two reminders? Or perhaps it was more, as the palm device rings every five minutes until it's fifteen minutes past the reminder time. My drive to have a more manageable inbox load to face on my first day back caused me to have tunnel vision (tunnel hearing, too, apparently).

I could let this cause a lot of doubt: "How could I have let this happen?" "Does it mean that I can no longer count on the computer and palm device reminders as task triggers?" "If this won't work, what the hell will?" "If I can't get this to work, how can I expect it to work for other people?"

Yes, all these thoughts are vying for attention.

The truth is, it's not the first time this has happened. There have been other times when I was so focused on something that I didn't hear the reminder alarms. But my experience has been that, for me, they work about 90% of the time.

Two more ideas pop into awareness:

1. I'm not perfect, and that's okay. If I can't admit that I'm not perfect, and that I do miss things or screw up from time to time, I'm not only putting an excessive amount of pressure on myself, I'm also lying! Being lenient with myself in this way does not mean I'm

courting failure and mediocrity. Quite the contrary. While my aim, focus, and drive is to always succeed, I can operate more effectively if I'm not afraid to fail. I'm actually more likely to be unsuccessful if my attention is on fear of failing rather than doing a wonderful job and enjoying it as much as I can.

2. There are other measures I can take to ensure that something is accomplished. While this particular mission is important, it isn't absolutely required that I start at 9:00 a.m. and finish at 10:00 a.m.. My schedule is flexible enough that I can start ten minutes late and finish ten minutes past the next hour. For more time/deadline oriented tasks, I can build in an "environment" that supports me and isn't so dependent on my own internal resources. Being late when you're presenting for a conference, for instance, is not an option, so a stronger structure is called for. That might include using my own alarm clock, the hotel's wake-up call, setting up my cell phone voicemail to call me with a reminder, or asking one of the conference organizers to knock on my door. I could also set the time somewhat earlier than I'd need in order to build in a cushion, lay out my clothes and materials the evening before, get to bed early enough the night before to be rested, delegate responsibilities and tasks to others so I don't get delayed by them, and create a timeline to follow to ensure all the bases have been covered.

July 13—9:19 a.m.

What caused me to be nineteen minutes late for this morning's writing? Partly it was that I was balancing my business books earlier this morning, and tidying up the house before a moving company estimator arrives in another hour or two. This cut into my scheduled shower.

This would have made me only about ten minutes late, but discussing some items with my husband interfered, and then the dual enticements of new emails to review and a website on moving scams threatened to distract me. I remained under their spells for only about one or two minutes each before realizing what I was doing.

I've found (for my clients as well as for myself) that it's very effective to create a schedule for the day, along with a list of three or four items you must accomplish, possibly adding another two or three you'd like to accomplish. It's been quite useful to schedule those to-do's into the day so you can complete them by the end the day rather than pushing them off until the next day.

Often, though, life intrudes. A call you've been waiting for comes in just when you were scheduled to start on a project; someone needs your help with something urgently; an unexpected priority project gets laid in your lap; in the midst of working on something you realize that there's something equally or more important that you need to take care of. This has been happening this morning! As I write this, I've already made four telephone calls, some of which I've been meaning to do for weeks—the kind of things you remember to do when in the shower but, for obvious reasons, can't write down at that moment, that haven't made it onto a list. It feels so good to get them off my plate.

It's when I'm focused enough to take a look at how the smaller, hour-by-hour aspect of my life is (or can be designed to be) aligned with the much bigger picture of how I live a contributory, grounded, and fulfilling life that I not only feel the best, but accomplish the most. Some days I'm too distracted by the appointments and administrative tasks that I have on my plate, the scheduling of which I know I need to continue to improve upon to allow enough psychic elbow room to connect daily with my longer term objectives.

Although it's common for me, it never ceases to amaze me how productive I am when I plan the day in advance and continually review it throughout the day. Not only did I accomplish all but one item on today's list (eight items, a number of which required composing text, working through details, and making decisions), but I added another four items as I moved through the day, all of which are done, and an additional large task which is in progress.

And there were numerous interruptions throughout the day. Yippee!

The one item I didn't complete (heck, I didn't even start it, really), I'll admit, I meant to do yesterday. And I'm committed to completing it tomorrow. It's a heavy schedule tomorrow, so I'll have to start the task at 7:00 a.m., and finish the details later. Because it's a packed day, my writing is slated for 7:00 p.m., so I hope to have this task completed by then, and be able to report (Ack! Accountability!) on it tomorrow.

July 14—9:15 p.m.

My energy is waning, but I've made a promise to myself that I'd be back having completed the task I committed to yesterday. While it's more than two hours later than planned, I had set up a system for myself that inspired me to make good on both the assignment and creating today's diary entry.

Just to turn the screws slightly tighter, I included

yesterday's diary entry in an e-newsletter that I sent out to my mailing list of over seven hundred people. At the end, of the entry, I invited readers to e-mail me to see if I'd fulfilled my promise. I made it *harder to procrastinate* than to get it done.

While I applied myself to this monthly chore early this morning, as I started on it I discovered that I needed more information from others, and sought it. That took more time, and they weren't immediately available, which caused additional delay. Because my calendar for the day was already full of appointments, there was no time to get to it until this evening. It took longer than expected, but it's completed. It motivated me to follow up on some details I'd thought about but hadn't done anything with.

Now I'm going to reward myself by getting to bed a little earlier than I might have to read a bit and ensure a good night's sleep.

July 15—9:02 a.m.

Wow, do I feel crappy today. This infection or cold, I'm not sure which it is, is in my chest and my energy level is really low.

This is a good day to revisit a paragraph from Don Miguel Ruiz's book, *The Four Agreements*, from the chapter titled "Always Do Your Best."

"Under any circumstance, always do your best, no more and no less. But keep in mind that your best is never going to be the same from one moment to the next. Everything is alive and changing all the time, so your best will sometimes be high quality, and other times it will not be as good. When you wake up refreshed and energized in the morning, your best will be different than when you are tired at night. Your best will be different when you are healthy as opposed to sick, or sober as opposed to drunk. Your best will depend on whether you are feeling wonderful and happy, or upset, angry or jealous."

It's unreasonable to expect very high quality today; it's a day to fulfill my obligations reasonably, without needing to be exemplary, and to take on no more than is already scheduled. Thankfully, while yesterday was rather intense, today's schedule is more forgiving.

It's one of those days when my concentration is a bit fractured, and I watch myself zigzagging from one activity to the next, making progress, but not in a cohesive way that completes the tasks. But that's alright for today. I'm still making progress. Since I started writing, I've paused to make about half a dozen necessary telephone calls, write five or six emails (feels so good that they're done!), and instant message a colleague about finding an assistant for a joint effort we're working on.

Recognizing that the hour is flying by, I return to this diary, to continue to chronicle my own particular story of how I'm carrying out my desire to continue to write this book with as little procrastination as possible.

July 19—9:14 a.m.

How could I have worked this morning out more efficiently? It's been quite the morning of mentally juggling priorities. Although I was up before six (and yes, I could have, and perhaps should have gotten up a few minutes earlier, but didn't), I made time to work out, walk the dog with my husband (quality time), shower, spend a little time birding, get a couple of loads of laundry in, and now it's 9:15 a.m.. I'm once again late for my writing appointment.

You may be asking yourself how birding (bird-watching) can be a priority.

Just after waking this morning I read a list of intentions I'd created for myself a few months ago. One of the intentions is to spend time birding or studying ornithology or bird behavior about four times per week (about an hour or more each time). During the previous couple of days, I had also thought about how infrequently I had been to Lake Tappan for the last two months, a lovely spot for which I purchased a season pass. Nor had I spent much time at all birding anywhere. I had been ignoring this passion for birding and focused my attention on work, chores, e-mail, and projects. Birding is something that is an energy enhancer. To include it in my life regularly gives me more "juice" in general. For me, a fulfilling life definitely includes birding.

It's been interesting to watch my own mental gymnastics as I compute how long this or that will take me, how much time I can spare for one thing or another. I returned from birding with five minutes to spare before this writing appointment with myself. But a load of laundry was waiting to be hung up to dry, and another load to go in. Being fussy in the care of my clothing, it took almost fifteen minutes to finish hanging it. Although I would like to have put it off until later, I am carving out an additional hour this morning for a simultaneous manicure/pedicure (and don't want to ruin the manicure by doing laundry before the nails are completely dry). "Another frivolity," my mind scolds.

I am not a "high maintenance gal." Self-care, however, is unwisely ignored, I've learned. And each person has their threshold or degree to which it is reasonable. My appearance to others in a business setting requires that I be well groomed, including hands and nails. Even more to the point, however, is that for the next week and a half, I will feel delight every time I look at my hands because their appearance is pleasing.

So, about two hours ago, as I was completing my shower/dressing routine, I spent some time weighing birding and manicure. Which was higher priority? Believe me, if I could snap my fingers and those fingers be magically re-manicured in that second, I'd do it! Both activities are a form of self-care, and it's been a challenge to me to incorporate good self-care habits. The lack of time spent birding over the past couple of months is evidence. I've also got quite a bit of reading that has accumulated. I love to read, but it feels indulgent when I do because I'm not "doing" anything. Currently, I don't even look at the newspapers all week, and I'm "lucky" if I get to them on the weekend. I almost never watch television, so I have little idea of what's going on in the world from day to day (thank goodness for CNN's important news e-mail alerts!).

After almost two weeks, my manicure is very shabby, and rather than delighting in my nails, I cringe when I look at them.

Knowing that investing myself in these things, rather than concentrating solely on work all of the time, brings me more success rather than less, and certainly more daily and moment-by-moment enjoyment in life, is what motivates me. There's a leap of faith I have to continually make to remove myself from investing exclusively in work (which, ironically, will keep me playing a smaller game, rather than a larger one), and to spend some time, energy, and money in enhancing my overall energy level for greater general effectiveness. This includes working in some of the less tangible pleasures that I deserve and desire, as well, of course, as the diet/exercise/sleep self-care that's foundational. If I'm coming from a place of being afraid to invest in this because I feel it will limit my success, even though I can "afford" to do so, when ever will I? It's ironic that this scarcity attitude could keep me from the very success I'm working so hard for.

Besides, if I don't take care of me, who will? What will it take for me to make a little more time for enjoyment?

When I mentioned the all things I'd already done this morning, before getting to this, I was feeling a bit better. While I make a game of how productive I can be, and play with my schedule in this experimental way, I do sometimes lose sight of that experimental and playful perspective. Paradoxically, my high standards are beginning have their sharp edges polished down by having a more expansive, or "bigger," standard and at the same time having that standard be somewhat forgiving and flexible.

July 20—9:06 a.m.

Despite opening the document right on time, I've allowed a minor delay of two telephone calls and an email. There's no wiggle room in my schedule this morning, so there will simply be fewer minutes spent in this activity. But I'm quite peaceful and calm about that. [The rest of the hour was spent on writing the book.]

July 23—10:00 a.m.

Yesterday I hosted/facilitated a telephone call that about a hundred and fifty people attended. The guests were Dr. Steve Levinson and Pete Greider, authors of the book *Following Through: A Revolutionary New Model for Finishing Whatever You Start.*

During the call, I was surprised, impressed, and fascinated when they were talking about how they are collaborating on a new book together and how getting down to the writing aspect was difficult and something they continually found themselves putting off.

If these experts on procrastination still find themselves procrastinating, what does that mean for the rest of us?

Their contention is that our human brain is faultily wired, because our good intentions are so often waylaid by our more pressing in-the-minute primal urges. So we have to pressure, squeeze, push, wheedle, and cajole ourselves into performance and follow-through.

There are aspects of this philosophy/approach that I agree with, but some that I don't. The notion that our brain wiring is faulty is an amusing and interesting conceit, but not one that makes much sense. In the end, if our brain wiring is faulty, how is it that we can successfully use our brain to create intentions that are powerful enough to provoke us to follow through and therefore defeat what is thought to be our brain's faulty wiring? To me this is faulty logic!

It's true of course that there's much that isn't logical when it comes to the brain, and to analyze and parse things ad infinitum can often be less useful than gazing at our navel. Levinson's and Greider's bemused stance that we have to put up with and make the most use of our less-than-perfect brains and bodies is admirable for its lightness and pressure-reducing perspective. However, it doesn't seem to account for people who have made permanent changes because they've been inspired by their positive intentions. Nor does it address how/why some of the coaching techniques my colleagues and I are using seem to dissolve competing aims so that pressuring, squeezing, pushing, wheedling, and cajoling often aren't necessary, or are at least secondary.

July 28—9:05 a.m.

Something that should be noted in this diary is that a gap between dates doesn't necessarily mean that I've missed my writing appointment with myself on those days, but is usually due to being away on business (or vacation), or to writing the meat of the book as opposed to writing a diary entry. Which is a good thing! Otherwise, I'll get caught up in the fun of relating how life may be altering the way I'm approaching this book and never complete it.

Right now, at this very moment, I notice my eyes straying to the telephone, even if for a half of a second. There is a call I want to make, and I'm so enticed to pick up the telephone.

Instead, to my surprise, the telephone actually rings. It's my mom, and she's going away, so I'd better take the call, as she may be gone if I wait to get back to her.

Fortunately, the details she needed didn't take much time, and it's one less thing I have to remember to do later. While it did cut into my writing time by a few minutes, it's minimal and nothing to be concerned about.

I'd scheduled this writing slot for 9:00 a.m. this morning. At that time, however, I was in the middle of a conversation with a colleague about some deadline-oriented tasks that needed completion. Since I had time later in the day, it seemed appropriate to adjust my schedule accordingly, and I rescheduled writing for the

4:30-5:30 p.m. slot.

At 4:40 pm I found myself in another room, away from my computer reminder, searching desperately for a disk with a file I'd created last month, somewhat anxious that the file hadn't gotten saved, and the work had been lost. I'd meant to forward the file a couple of weeks ago, and hadn't gotten to it, also neglecting to write down that detail for later completion. I didn't want to forget again, and didn't want to waste time looking in the same places again later. Aware that I had a 6:00 p.m. appointment, I again bumped my writing appointment up to 5:00 p.m.

Oh, the little unexpected things that throw a monkey wrench into our schedules! It took almost an hour of searching, something that rarely happens to me, but happened this time, embarrassingly enough—after all, for years I did teach a course titled "Find It in a Minute—Or Less!", but I located the file. Relieved, and having forwarded the file successfully, it was just moments after 5:00 p.m. when I opened this diary for a new entry.

In the past, I might have spent a fair amount of energy on any or all of the following:

- being upset with myself for not having found the file more quickly
- being angry with myself that I allowed my schedule to be altered
- being frustrated that so much of my time got used looking for something
- being embarrassed that it took me, the queen of organization, so long to find something (this is similar, but slightly different than the first item)
- being aggravated that I haven't gotten as much done today as I would have liked

Instead, there's an inner chuckle and surrender to the fact that the situation simply is as it is, rather than any of the above.

As I finish writing the above, my eyes glance at the clock. Only 5:34 p.m. I still have twenty-six minutes to write. There is a sensation of both excitement (that I have more time to write) and apprehension (that I have more time to write!). For a brief moment, I consider doing something else. My commitment to completing this book wins out. And so, back to the book.

August 3—8:08 a.m.

It's one of those "I don't feel like working today" mornings. Last night I returned from a trip to the site of my new home, where I took care of getting a new driver's license, post office box, registering to vote, opening a checking account, looking for temporary housing while the home is being built, and meeting with the builder, among other things. As I didn't get back until after 10:00 p.m., I decided to wait until this morning to go through the mail, download and read e-mail, and look at my telephone messages. At times this delaying until morning would have been difficult, but it wasn't last night because of the whirlwind errand-running I'd done while being away.

This morning, however, as I was somewhat tempted to start looking through and responding to e-mail first thing, after a workout and walking the dog, I found myself going to the kitchen to have something to eat. For most people, this is natural. For me, recently, this is a rarity.

Earlier, at about 7:20 a.m., my husband had so kindly

booted up the computer, and e-mail was downloading when I sat in front of the monitor to look at the day's schedule, right before getting in the shower. As it continued to download, instead of taking a quick shower, echoes of my husband telling me that "I bought some nice-looking bananas and I hope you'll share them with me" was luring me to the kitchen. Unremittingly, e-mail was still downloading as I returned with the banana, and without plan, I was back in the kitchen, pulling out ingredients for more of a breakfast. I pulled out a knife to start slicing some tomatoes and noticed it was dull. As I then pulled out the knife-sharpening appliance, my mind was asking why I was spending time on this instead of weeding through e-mail (545 messages since Friday morning and it's now Tuesday morning—I'm hoping many of them are spam!). Yet I continued with this mission until my husband returned and offered to make me breakfast.

Rather than return to the office, instead I sorted through the three days worth of mail that had accumulated, recycling much of it, and working my through the rest.

For the last year or more, if I eat breakfast, I usually eat it in front of my monitor while working. Yes, for most people this isn't the most optimal way to start the day. My day, however, usually starts a couple of hours before I get to the office, and I'm usually reading e-mail while eating, much like eating and reading the newspaper. Today, though, I went into the sunroom to look through some catalogs that had arrived in the mail instead. When the writing appointment reminder rang at 8:00 a.m. I grudgingly acknowledged it, but didn't move from my catalog reviewing for another few minutes. Perhaps if I just accepted that I'm in a rebellious mood, it might help. In spite of that, though, here I sit, typing away, the only thing I've truly postponed so far this morning is a shower. It will have to wait for another hour and a half. These are the merits of working from home.

August 6—9:08 a.m.

Hmm, something happened with my computer, and I lost yesterday's entry. That's disappointing! I'd missed writing entirely on the 4th, having had a morning appointment with myself that got shuffled to later that day because of business priorities, and then got shuffled again to later in the evening due to personal moving issues. By the time that appointment arrived, I no longer had the energy or focus to write. While I could have forced myself, the product would have been poor.

Yesterday's entry began with relating how all this happened. Some would say it was a story justifying my lack of follow-through the day before. I could certainly agree, and would have in the past. My experience, both with myself and with my clients, proves that while holding oneself to a higher standard can be a good thing, it's wise to know when to be flexible and let yourself off the hook when it's appropriate.

Much of my housing plans for the next four or five months is now up in the air, requiring research and decision-making. To spare the boring details, I'll just say for various reasons that our plans to move to our New York home for three to five months have suddenly been supplanted by a probable plan to move to New York for two weeks, and then into temporary housing in Florida. And all this will be happening in just over a week. I am generally not a particularly impulsive or spontaneous person, so this abrupt change in plans is not made lightly.

This turn of events has required not only extra time to research and consider our options, as well as think about what we must have in place for our move, but the practical ramifications of the change. It makes me want to pause at this task for the moment to create a list of what details will be needed in each place. Excuse me for a moment.

I'm back. It took only a few minutes to start creating the list, and while it's not complete, I've "downloaded" some of the tasks onto paper so my head can remain clearer.

What I realized is that there has been an unexpected shift in plans, and therefore in priorities. With just over a week left before our move, these new probable plans, which are still not yet firm, have necessitated a shift in how I allocate my time, and they are also something that will require attention and energy, leaving less for some other things I'd like to be doing, like making strong progress with this book in the next few weeks as all of this transpires.

That's not to say, though, that I'm willing to put off writing entirely for the next month or so. Rather, it will be on a back burner rather than off the stove for the time being.

August 10—10:10 a.m.

It was very tempting to put off this writing appointment entirely. Having spent all day yesterday weeding through belongings, lifting heavy boxes in confined spaces, piling old belongings up for a tag sale, and packing up what is to be moved, my body is a little tired. I skipped writing yesterday, though that was planned. And I'm a little drained by plans being up in the air: yesterday evening the option to move later in the month came up. This is a decision that has to be made in the next twenty-four hours, and it is using up a good portion of the "back of my brain" as I consider the pros, cons, ramifications, and logistics of the two options.

Added to the mix is the juggling of address changes (my old address here, the summer address in NY, the post office box address in FL, a new rental address in FL, and my eventual primary address in FL), arranging the turning off and on of various utilities for three residences, continuing to weed my belongings in the next few days, and my regular business activities.

I expect there will be some things that fall through the cracks, and I've made sure to warn my clients, business associates, friends, family, and neighbors of this so they're not too dismayed when and if it happens. Superwoman I am not, and it's a lot more comfortable to not try to be.

August 11—9:35 a.m.

For the past couple of days some of my work with a coach training organization has been intentionally set aside because I've been focusing more on the upcoming set of household moves and what is needed for them. Yesterday afternoon and evening my e-mail inbox was growing to amounts that had the potential to overwhelm me. Rather than let it do that, I simply focused on reducing the number of emails by ruthlessly deleting everything not necessary and important, using the Auto Preview feature in Outlook to see the subject and first line or two of the e-mail without actually opening any of them. This reduced the load by at least half. Then I concentrated on only the most important emails that also had the highest urgency.

A number of calls and appointments cut into my time for e-mail yesterday, so I made time after I returned from a goodbye dinner some friends threw for me. By 10:45 p.m. I had had enough, even though there were still well over forty unread emails remaining in the inbox. I would deal them in the morning.

This morning's schedule has allowed little time to review them, as well as all of the other emails that have arrived since then, though I did spend just a couple of minutes deleting the obvious spam and non-essential posts.

As this writing appointment rolled around, I was finishing up a call with an associate during which we were brainstorming around some current challenges. In the moment (and also in hindsight...half an hour later) it seemed more of a priority to complete the action plan for the needs she and I were discussing than get off quickly so I could keep my writing appointment. And part of that action plan was to immediately send off a couple of emails to others to get some balls rolling. One thing I did do, however, was to open this document, so it would be visible as a reminder.

It was twenty-three minutes after the hour by the time I completed sending those emails, and the remaining sixty-six unread emails in the inbox were beckoning. It was with some effort that I resisted them and instead trained my focus on this diary.

At first, I stared at the blank page, and that old sensation of "there's nothing there to write about!" and "nothing I have to say is going to be valuable for others" started to creep in. I continued to stare at the imposing white screen, though, long enough to allow that sensation to be recognized and then depart, freeing me to relate these last few paragraphs.

August 13—8:42 a.m.

In preparation for the first phase of our move, my computer has been moved, and everything is in disarray. In spite of that, there's some ironic delight that the desk I now find myself working at is a much nicer and more comfortable space.

There's pressure to have everything in order for this move, and concern in the degree of preparation for it. It's prompted me to spend some extra time this morning reviewing some of the areas I hadn't yet really tackled. While I'm not a lot further on them, the time spent caused delay and resulted in my being late to this writing appointment. That's understandable in these circumstances. My deadline for completion of this book is not written in stone. There is nobody and nothing else compelling me to finish it. At the same time, I refuse to let it slide completely during the move.

As I sit here surrounded by chaos, many things are drawing my attention for action. The phone ringing, the thank you notes needing to be written in acknowledgement of goodbye gifts given to me, the few bookkeeping entries that would be helpful to be made before the move, the utilities hookups that need to be arranged are just a few.

My schedule is packed again today, and on checking it, I notice that I have a half hour time slot from 9:00-9:30 a.m. that hasn't gotten anything scheduled. Do I use it to continue to write? Do I stop at 9:00 a.m. accomplishing some of the details listed above? Do I use the time, instead, to continue going through my possessions to feel more prepared for the move? It would be easy to feel overwhelmed. It would also be easy to feel plagued by a sense that no matter what I choose to do, I should be doing something else.

What is most important now are answering these questions: What is the highest and best use of my time that is in accordance with my long-term objectives? What do I need to know to use my time optimally and not let those niggling doubts drain my energy and momentum?

I've spent the last few moments stopping and being still, checking in with myself about what is most important. The knowledge that I accessed was that being prepared for the move so that it goes smoothly and allows me to be up and running again quickly during the various phases of the move is more important than spending the next half hour writing.

After this morning, it will be a week or more until I can get back to these writing appointments, which doesn't feel entirely comfortable, but it must be that way for now.

August 26
It's been an interesting, hectic, very disruptive two weeks, and now I'm back to my writing schedule. This doesn't feel altogether comfortable. I'm still not immune to the sense that I could push myself harder, and be more productive and on top of things. This is directly in conflict with other senses that inform me that it's important to take better-than-usual care of myself right now during this time of disorder, interruption, change, and transition. For

me that has meant going to bed earlier and getting up later, working effectively but not at my usual super-swift pace, (mostly) forgiving myself for the things I am not able to accomplish, and being grateful for what I am accomplishing.

There are a lot of personal/life/home details to attend to. More than the many I usually handle. My experience is that when I am entirely focused on my work, those details aren't attended to properly, if at all. I get so caught up that I don't pay attention to the rest of my life. That's never a useful pattern to fall into. Right now, though, it could really gum up the works. If I procrastinate, even by benign neglect, to call a pest control company to spray for carpenter ants, to contact the cable company to return the cable boxes before I leave for winter, to pack up what needs to come with us on the next leg of our move and pack away what needs to stay, to make sure all the documents are in order for the closing on our house, to attend to the dozens of other loose ends that need to be tied up, it will cost me. I'll pay not only in money, but in stress, frustration, worry, and most importantly, time.

One thing that happens when transitions like this occur is that habits often get broken. I haven't been untouched by this tendency. I haven't worked out in two weeks. I haven't been planning my days at the beginning of each day and, indeed, not even printing out the day's calendar each day; this makes things feel very haphazard, something that I'll address by getting back to these habits tomorrow.

The paradox of all of this is I'm able to enjoy this transition and not feel so stressed by it, that my slower pace, and the relaxing of standards, allows for a flexibility that lowers the tension in what could be a very nerve-racking period. It's my intention, though, to increase the pace and raise the standards. The challenge to improve, increase, and enhance is still inspiring and motivating me.

August 31—8:16 a.m.

Even though this is the day of the first leg of our move, and the computer I'm using to create this document must be packed up in a couple of hours, the attraction of knowing I'm making progress in the midst of this is too enticing to ignore.

Though I had scheduled this for 8:00 a.m., there was an interruption. The contractor who is repairing the porch here had arrived, and brought his young daughter, who wanted to play with our dog. It was appropriate to supervise them for a time to be sure that both of them would be safe and play well together. It was 8:06 when my cell phone rang. It was upstairs and I ran to get it but didn't reach it in time. The young girl called from downstairs. She wanted to play the organ and so I went to show her how to do it. The cell phone rang once again. It was the mover. He wants to move our things in a little earlier than we expected.

This, however, may be something of a problem. The house we're moving into for the next few months still has no electric meter; a hurricane knocked out electrical power across a widespread area and the utility wasn't installing any new electric meters until all power was restored. The county won't give a certificate of occupancy, and the landlord can't close until that is issued. Nor would we be able to move our things into the house until the c.o. is issued. We're hoping and praying that the meter gets installed today, and that they can close tomorrow. Earlier might be better, in that case, because there's another twist on the horizon. Literally!

Another large hurricane is headed toward the Atlantic coast of Florida, and may require evacuation. It's still days away, and we'll be watching it closely, but we may have to evacuate the house we've just moved into if the hurricane continues on its current track.

At any rate, these things are swirling in my head, acting as something of a distraction—as is the heavy hammering of the carpenters working on the porch just below me. For the fun of it, I'll try concentrating now on the body of this book and see how I do.

September 7

I made progress writing the other day, though not of the quality it sometimes is. That's fine. It was a useful experiment.

I could use the distraction of being in what feels like suspended animation as a rationalization, and it would do in a pinch. I could realize that it didn't even occur to me that I could spend more time writing until a few days ago. I could acknowledge that I've spent an awful lot of time watching The Weather Channel to see what the various hurricanes are doing and juggle my options. I could accept that there have been lots of small details to attend to, and that they've taken some time and effort.

Rather than beat myself up for not spending as much time writing during this period as I "could" have I could use it to look for what's right, as well as the opportunities present in the situation.

What is right?

- I didn't have to be in Florida for Hurricane Frances.
- I was able to spend some quality time with my mom while staying at her house and have learned to appreciate her even more.
- I got to visit two different sets of aunts and uncles on two occasions, and even help out one of them.
- I helped my mom choose and buy a new refrigerator (she needed one and likely wouldn't have done it on her own at this time).
- Since all of my business clothes are in storage, and I may not get them before an important business presentation, I bought a great new set of outfits that I'm delighted with.
- While this transition has been time-consuming, expensive, inconvenient, and is still unresolved, it allows me to be thankful that I have so many systems, practices, reserves, and structures in place so that I can weather it essentially unscathed.
- I have developed more faith in my ability to practice flexibility and openness (which is a substantial accomplishment for a former control freak).

What opportunities are present in this situation?

- It's a fun and interesting story to live through and be able to tell to clients and audiences; I've already started working it in to one of my presentations.
- This limbo-time can be used to write and to create

a new and superb presentation.

- Because such a substantial portion of my possessions and conveniences have been (and continue to be) in storage, I can appreciate and be grateful for how useful and treasured some of them are, as well as appreciate how little I really need.
- This has been an opportunity to ask for help from others, which is not something I'm practiced at doing but is, appropriately done, a way to accept providence and take advantage of circumstances or potential results that might otherwise be lost.

September 27—11:00 a.m.

Almost three weeks have gone by, and it oddly seems both like months and only a few days. After the long drive down, the stay in the hotel, the days without phone or cable service (or a desk!), without office supplies, the business trip to Hilton Head, the lengthy move-in followed by preparations for Hurricane Jeanne, I'm finally back at the computer for a writing appointment.

While there are still many things to take care of, many loose ends to tie up, at least now I have the equipment, the lack of distractions and other big priorities, and the focus to write.

Time seems to pass more quickly here!

Through this move it's helped give me enough distance from my regular work to recognize where I'm out of alignment with my long-term priorities, where I'm making choices that give some short-term reward but that are slowing my progress toward those things that will feel more significantly fulfilling.

And at the same time, I'm more able to acknowledge

that whatever I'm doing, it's "perfect," the best I am able to do at this time, and the opportunity to learn some valuable points from this detour.

Now it's time to write meatier matter...

September 28—4:17 p.m.

I admit it. I've been dawdling today. Not that I haven't been productive, but I *have* been putting off my writing appointment. While I have been attending to important tasks, there have been unimportant ones that I've placed before this one. Now, with just under forty-five minutes until a teleconference I must lead, I'm feeling more motivated to pursue writing, because if I don't do it now, it's unlikely I'll do it at all today.

In his book *!Inspire!,* Lance Secretan makes a distinction between motivation and inspiration. He contends that motivation derives from fear; inspiration from a more divine origin; that motivation is externally driven and is self-serving, whereas inspiration is generated from within and is other-serving.

My motivation derives both from the concern that I will somehow be less than credible or worthy if I don't stick to my writing schedule, but there is also inspiration in the form of the desire to complete this project and get this (hopefully uplifting and empowering) work out to the public.

September 29—8:04 a.m.

The classic silhouettes and stunning number of choices at Bernhardt Furniture's website held me rapt for the last ten minutes, eating slightly into my writing schedule. I watched myself as I allowed it to happen; it was, simply enough, the excitement and pleasure of pondering possible new couches which was pulling me away from something more taxing. As I clicked through all fourteen pages displaying nine models per page, briefly evaluating each, I wondered how quickly I could view all fourteen pages, and how late that would make me for this writing appointment. Today, the four minutes was worth it.

There are plenty of other things that have been put off, or rather that I've thought of many times but haven't yet put onto a to-do list: getting my hair trimmed, finding an insurance agent in this new location, going birding, scrubbing the insects off the front of my car before they ruin the finish, completing the list of items missing and damaged from the move for insurance claim purposes, finding out if we need to change health insurance since we've relocated.

These things will come in due time, as they develop into more of a priority.

What is important that isn't getting done? That's the real question. What's important?

Continuing to clarify and utilize as much of my potential as possible to affect the world in a positive way.

There are other important things, but nothing as important as that. The bills still need to get paid, the details still need attending to, but these can be managed so as not to interfere with or overwhelm the continual development and refinement of this potential.

Writing this book is an activity directed toward the development.

September 30—10:04 a.m.

As I made the mistake of drinking caffeinated coffee late in the day yesterday (what was I thinking?), sleep was fitful, and I'm grateful that I haven't a full schedule this morning. So I've tended to some calls and some emails rather than start writing directly at 9:00 a.m. It's a lovely luxury to not have a packed calendar every day.

Finally, earlier this morning, I got myself back on track with both exercise and birding. It was probably close to two months that the move and its necessities and priorities pulled me away from my routine and normal set-up. I was without a private indoor workout space, and while I did walk (jogging and I don't get along, and I have no bicycle at this time) I was too distracted by details to construct a whole new exercise habit.

And the thing about getting out there and birding is…well, I can't persuade God to give me any more than one sunrise per day. Since the birds are most active at that time, and it's also the time that Gracie is habitually walked, there's a conflict there, as dog walking and birding, at least the kind of birding that really does it for me, are pretty mutually exclusive. The former is about exercising the dog and giving her attention. The latter is about exercising my connection to all things, which requires silence and stillness.

But this morning I used an old exercise routine that I hadn't used in years, which doesn't require much space, walked the dog pre-sunrise, and went to the lake to bird just as the sun was rising over the trees. It was a perfectly delightful first-time birding adventure here in our new home.

That feels like an accomplishment.

October 7—10:39 a.m.

Well, it finally happened. I missed my writing appointment yesterday, one for which there was no more important justification for missing, and it was due purely to the typical reasons that most people attribute to their procrastination: things came up, I got involved in other details, I kept thinking I'd do it later but when later came I conveniently found other things to do.

While most of the time the absence of deadlines and accountability aren't an excuse not to keep to this commitment, yesterday they probably would have helped immensely.

Which brings me to a thought: perhaps it would be useful to take my own advice and seek out someone else, a buddy, with a related regular daily long-term project.

October 13

It's surprising. Now that things are settling down, and it would seem like there's both more psychic space as well as space on my schedule to keep my writing appointments, I have failed to do so for the previous two days. This comes at a time when I've been applying myself to finding a project buddy as a helpful strategy.

Which, to my mind, is evidence that I need to look, once again, a bit deeper into the reasons I've been holding in my mind as to what I'm getting out of writing this book, and the expectations I have about how and when it will be completed.

Rather than examine what I eventually hope to get out of writing, maybe it will be more productive to ask what I'm getting out of it now, since I'm writing it now. Aside from the very small ego-boost of telling other people I'm writing a book (and in this age of self-publishing, who isn't these days?), it's an opportunity to put my own concepts, beliefs, and work with others to test in a laboratory that is visible to others, for their scrutiny (oh, just a little bit of pressure there!). It will provide me with a time and mental space for self-expression that may be harder to come by elsewhere. It is an experiment that I'm playing with, which I can have fun with or ruin by taking too seriously. It's a way to really put myself out there in a more expansive way, for myself alone at this time, and eventually, if I choose, to a much larger audience.

Some books write themselves. The author almost can't help herself as the words flow out. There is a message or story which feels unstoppable and is almost as if channeled.

Other books are carefully constructed, as though each sentence was a brick, each chapter a room, all skillfully laid out on a thoroughly pre-planned and measured foundation.

Yet other books are an assemblage of thoughts, tales, theories, or sermons on a central theme, created over time and woven together at a later date.

I just now realized there is something affecting my approach to writing this diary: a friend of mine who has written and edited books responded to a diary entry I had put in my e-mail newsletter this way:

"As an editor and professional book packager, I wonder how you are planning to develop your procrastination diary. It partakes of the contemporary taste for original detail, and the unemotional, self-observational, cinema-verite genre. Knowing you, the whole will be greater than its parts. That is, without becoming preachy or didactic, I imagine some larger truth or more abiding vision emerging from the relentless self-scrutiny. Still, there is the problem of keeping the

readers' attention throughout without getting either too humdrum or gimmicky. An interesting challenge for sure and I for one, am eager to stay tuned."

Groan. That's a critical voice that's been circling in my head, dogging every sentence, acting like a lead anchor on my energy to keep making diary entries.

October 18—6:38 p.m.

Re-reading her comment, it's obvious that I've taken it as something of a warning, and have felt intimidated by its implications ever since, without being aware of it. Its subtle pressure and high standards have been niggling, draining, and hurdle-inducing.

More drag has been generating, as well, from other reading I've been doing about publishing a book, such as needing a strong and well-developed marketing plan, a large contact database, and a firmly established "platform" (media and public visibility structure, such as a magazine or television affiliation, a large established readership). Seems you've already got to be fairly famous and have a relatively wide-ranging audience to attract a publisher.

While I'm well known in coaching industry circles, it's not a large number of people.

Add to that the time and effort it takes for the editing process and the rigor and discipline that it requires, and it seems positively mountainous. I've spent much of the last week in the shadows of that mountain without having much clarity that I was, or why. It seems like it's the same old story, but now I've gotten down to more brass tacks about where it's been coming from. On top of that, it takes a while to let go of the almost automatic return to the deeply entrenched critical patterns and firmly replace them with more quickly available productive patterns.

So now that some new information has been uncovered…what do I do about it?

Same as in the past: I continue with both the book itself, as well as the diary. I have little to lose and a lot to gain. There will be at least something of an audience for this book, even if it's only my clients and presentation audiences, industry conference bookstores, prospects, and through my websites (hmm, I can see I'm already getting little more psyched about how this book will get out into the world). Self-publishing through a number of reputable firms is not out of my reach, and can be a good start. Publishing as an e-book is another option.

There will be some who find this diary dull or an irritating exercise in "relentless self-scrutiny," or "humdrum or gimmicky." Let them. Allowing that possibility to slow or stop me, as it has done, is not what I want for myself.

Meanwhile, the search for a buddy continues.

November 9

Woe is me. Data—writing, that is—has been lost. Some bug in my computer closed down Word's functionality and I've lost a few days worth of writing due to mistakenly deleting some of the recovered files.

All the reworking of the table of contents, new chapter content, and diary entries have been lost.

I'm not going to cry over it. I already have a headache and that would only make it worse. I'm just glad it was only a few days worth of data. And I'll hit the save key more often, you can bet on it.

The week before last I went to a workshop at which I

had hoped to meet or be put in contact with a project buddy. While I put out feelers, nothing much has happened so far. However, at last week's International Coach Federation annual conference, and in the day I've been back, there have been a number of possible avenues for finding someone. I'm in the process of following up and looking forward to seeing what shakes out.

Meanwhile, the plan is in place to create a book proposal so that I can start shopping it around. As the book is almost 50% completed (at least that's a current estimate), I hope to have a contract by the time I'm done with it.

Which brings to mind the fact (and there's no way around this fact) that I haven't been writing as much as I had planned. This doesn't please me. At the same time, however, I've had three business trips in the last two weeks, and I recognize that it's time to put some effort into creating a book proposal. While I had originally figured on self-publishing (and may still end up going that route for a first printing), I believe it may be more beneficial to go with a traditional publisher. If nothing else, creating a book proposal is a good exercise to engage in to get very clear and succinct regarding what the book is about, who it is for, how it will be positioned, who the competition is, and why it deserves to be published. It requires you to continue to be a leading and cutting-edge authority on your subject, which requires you to continue researching what others in your field are doing.

And hey, I get to use the excuse that I'm putting my efforts into the proposal and research areas instead of writing! What a great rationalization.

Kidding…

I plan to do it all at the same time, using each piece to inform and polish the others.

November 11—9:27 a.m.

While I've had success in attracting some potential project buddies, I didn't anticipate having to turn people down because they don't fit as well as others. I don't know whether taking on more than one project buddy will be helpful or distracting.

There has been a pause…what is it that I want to relate? Why am I not coming up with something? At the moment I stop long enough to relax into this inquiry rather than resist its presence, I realize that some negative course feedback from a recent telephone conference class (which was plagued by telephone bridge issues) is playing into my "come from." I recognize that there are mobius loop tapes playing in the background of my awareness, telling me that, try as I might, the value of what I produce is limited; that the quality of my work is not up to snuff.

Rather than avoid the sensation this brings up (so very pleasant…NOT!), I ease into it. I look at the sky, focusing intently on the blue rather than the clouds. This allows my thoughts to settle, and puts me in a more relaxed state where measuring up isn't a concern. It prepares me to recognize where I'm holding the tension of this sensation. I locate its center in my sternum. It feels like a hand is squeezing my soul. My attention directed toward its nexus, I take a deep breath and sense heaviness and a dull ache. Another deep breath and I notice how the rest of me feels: my heartbeat pulsing in my hands resting in my lap, the weight of my thighs in the chair, the muscle tension in my neck with my shoulders slightly pulled up and my head uncomfortably positioned in relation to my spine.

Relaxing my shoulders and focusing on the energy of this tension, the hand feels like it begins to open, the pressure eases, and it no longer feels like I'm in its grip. Opening my eyes, it feels like there's no longer friction between my focus and what needs to be accomplished.

November 16—8:07 a.m.

I'm now working with not only one, not just two, but no less than three project buddies. There were a number of people who stepped forward, and a few of them were promising. In order to ultimately choose the most fitting person, these alliances are arranged on a two-week trial basis. This will allow time to see what works out and shakes out. It may be that the connection, chemistry, or direction one or two of the people want to go in does not match me well.

The book proposal has been started; the first draft of the overview and target market sections have been written. Some statistics were needed for the target market section, and I found some promising resources there. Today's task is to review these resources so that I can continue to have the most up-to-date information about what's going on in the field. I may even contact one of the people who is doing some research in the area to see if he'd be open to a discussion.

November 17—9:02 a.m.

While it wouldn't be unexpected, it's a bit of a surprise that my buddy sessions are lasting longer than planned. This first week I can allow for that, this being a trial run with all three buddies. I'm already getting an idea who will be the best candidate.

Yesterday's research was conducted but curtailed earlier than planned due to numerous phone calls, important tasks (paying bills, reconciling accounts, updating accounting data), and completing details that had been hanging around and distracting my focus. Even though I've experienced and have been preaching about it for years, it never ceases to amaze me how a disorderly desk can fracture one's clarity and attention.

It was nighttime before I got around to contacting procrastination researcher Piers Steel for a book endorsement, via e-mail, as it was too late to call. But I did put it out there, and it will be fascinating to see if he responds (or procrastinates in responding!).

November 19

Dr. Steel was actually quite prompt in responding. However, as he says he not only has a patent pending, but also a book offer in the works, he is not open at this time to a correspondence or discussion. This news, that he may well be writing a book on procrastination, caused me concern, and had the potential to slow me down a bit in my progress. After all, he's a university professor with a doctoral degree and he's read every research paper on procrastination; isn't he much more credible a source of procrastination advice than I? And his website shows that his writing style is accessible and entertaining. Uh oh!

Seeing this potential downward spiral (and impending procrastination) starting to gather momentum, and not wanting it to do so, I contacted a few colleagues to reach out for more objective support. Even more effectively, I made the concern a focus of a call with my own coach. This helped give me a larger perspective and more possibilities than I could come up with on my own, and got me out of thinking, "His patent pending and possible book will completely eclipse my efforts, and I will be seen as a quack. All this time and work will have been a waste, and I'm going to have to pick a new field and get very well educated in it, possibly pursuing a doctoral degree."

About six months ago, a growing thought erupted into a possible action plan that I should enroll in an accredited doctoral program. I looked into it and found an institution that would enroll me, and was sincerely considering it. The cost was significant, but more than that, it was a three-to-five-year effort that would take a lot of my time. Was I willing, at this point in my life, to devote that much of my life-energy into obtaining this degree? What did the degree mean, and why did I think I needed it? I had bought into (and to some extent still do buy into) the idea that you're a lot less authoritative an expert if you don't have Dr. at the front of your name or Ph.D. at the end of it. Certainly, there are many people who also believe this, and that was a reason. It does add to your marketability. It's true that you're much more likely to know what you're talking about if you've had to write and defend a dissertation! I also have a value and love of learning, and if you're preparing for or writing a dissertation it's likely you'll be learning a lot.

On the other hand, there are plenty of people who are considered a specialist or consummate professional in their field who do not have doctoral degrees. What might I be able to accomplish, or how might I be able to apply myself if I was not putting so much into obtaining a more advanced degree? Did I want to have this long-term obligation and would I be enjoying my life during it? In the end, after the three to five years was over, would I have been able to establish myself as a known and visible expert by other means, or would I still have to go on a public relations campaign to do it? Even if I conducted that campaign during the process, would I be that much further ahead by having the degree?

After much consideration, I decided to put the idea aside, at least for the current year. I've classified this large "to-do" as falling into the "not the right goal" category of productive procrastination.

Back to my e-mail from Dr. Steel, and its possible effect on me. Before I sought others' outlook on the situation, it was hard for me to have a more expanded view. It was hard to see the forest for the trees. Once I had a few conversations with others, though, their ideas and angles of approach gave me a broader understanding of, and openness to, how there might be room for both Dr. Steel and me in the procrastination market.

December 12—6:19 p.m.

While it's been a while since I've made an entry, that doesn't mean I've been procrastinating! I've been putting together the proposal for this book, reading a number of other books on the market about procrastination, creating a procrastination survey, and adding pages and ideas to the body of the book.

My buddy system, which I've been using for almost a month now, is working very well to help keep me goal-oriented on the day-to-day progress that will lead to completion of the book, shopping the proposal around to an agent and then an editor, editing it, getting it published, and then getting it out into the world. Having that structure each day in the form of a ten-minute telephone call to report our progress and commit to a goal until we next speak (every weekday with one buddy, Mon/Wed/Fri with the other) has been helpful in many ways.

My buddies are two women I very much respect. One is a clinical instructor for Harvard as well as a published author who has a six-figure advance on the book she's writing (her project for this buddying go-round), and the other is a successful consultant, trainer, and coach. Aside from the accountability (I'd be embarrassed to report if I didn't do what I'd committed to) we share helpful ideas, resources, congratulate each other on our progress, provide a fresh eye (and ear), and it's fun simply to be in touch with them in this way. I didn't know either of them much before this began, and it's been a pleasure getting to know more about who they are and what they're like, as well.

There had been one thing that has been niggling recently, and I couldn't put my finger on it until I had a conversation with some colleagues. There was something holding me back in some way, not allowing me to be quite as inspired as I wished, and speaking to these colleagues helped pinpoint it. What it took was simply a willingness to explore, by thinking out loud, various ideas until the issue rose to the surface. Once identified, it could then be addressed, and no longer cause the minor energy leakage it had been costing.

January 5—4:44 p.m.

I'd make an appointment to start writing today at 3:30 p.m. It's now 4:44, and I'm just starting. I have an appointment in fifteen minutes. How adroitly I've avoided writing today!

Of course, there were the usual, and some unusual

tasks and interruptions that got in the way, but I'm curious about what might really be going on here. Excuse me a moment while I take a few seconds to check in with myself.

Okay, here it is. I've got a lot of good rationalizations for why I haven't concentrated on writing today: I'm having a party in about two hours, and there will be thirty to forty people here, possibly more. There are lots of details regarding work and building the house that have come to a head and need to be dealt with. And I've wanted to put some of them in some sort of order, as well as get some of them out of the way.

That's all well and good, productive, and useful. However, there's little cushion for me today to fall back upon in terms of getting writing done later. And here I sit and compose this entry (well, this was on the goals list for today).

Eight minutes until my appointment. I'm going to spend it writing the book! While I think I might get to it after the party, I'm guessing I'll be exhausted. But…you never know. Here's another commitment: I'll write in this diary tomorrow as to whether I succeed or not.

January 6

I got over half a page written…certainly a worthwhile effort.

January 17—8:45 a.m.

While it's about thirty minutes past my writing appointment today, it's pillows that have delayed me. Yes, pillows.

Yesterday morning I had laundered the mattress and pillow covers on our bed and recognized how badly we need new pillows. I wanted to order them online, but because I didn't write it down, I couldn't remember what I wanted to order. Until this morning.

So I've been on a web pillow search (latex foam is my preference, and I saved $120 on three pillows by shopping around, much less than it would have taken to comparison shop at "bricks and mortar" stores). And that's a good thing. But I have an appointment in ten minutes with one of my buddies, and this is all I've written. It's quite short of a full page.

Eight minutes left. I'm gonna blast out another half page of the body of the book in that time!

9:14 a.m.

Well, I did get two paragraphs written, plus what I've written above. While it's not a full page, it was a good effort. And I'm going to adjust my schedule a bit to write more this afternoon, which will give me more "make up" time to cover the thirty minutes lost earlier. I may end up spending more time, rather than less.

January 19—3:59 p.m.

It was unrealistic to expect that I'd keep my writing appointment this morning; there was just too much going on. This afternoon a telephone call cut into my writing. It was a scheduled call and took longer than planned, mostly because of the social aspect of the call, i.e., catching up with the person. I've been learning these past few years that relationships are more important than results. It's been a long lesson for me, and one I still sometime struggle with, as I'm so very results-oriented. Today, the relationship took precedent over the result (getting another page written). I still have another forty-five minutes though, and may take advantage of it.

Next door, however (literally a few feet away), there is a piece of earth-moving equipment making lots of loud noise and literally shaking the ground under my house. It's not easy to concentrate. I could go into a whole self-critical tirade (I can sense murmurs of it at the edges of my mind) about how if I'd gotten my goal accomplished earlier I wouldn't be in this position now. But I'm not going there.

And miraculously, the earth-moving equipment has moved on to some other piece of earth farther away. I can still hear the rumbling, but it's not as distracting. A good opportunity to spend the next minutes writing.

Bibliography

Burka, Jane B. *The Procrastination Cure*. [Sound recording (abridged audio book)] Chicago, IL: Nightingale-Conant, 1989.

Burka, Jane B. *Procrastination: Why You Do It, What To Do About It*. Reading, MA: Addison Wesley Pub. Co., c1983.

Douglass, Merrill E., Baker, Larry D. *The New Time Management: What Will You Accomplish With Two Extra Hours Every Day?* [Sound recording] Nightingale-Conant; Toms River, NJ, 1983.

Emmett, Rita. *The Procrastinator's Handbook: Mastering the Art of Doing It Now*. [Sound recording (abridged audio book)]: Los Angeles, CA: Audio Renaissance, 2001.

Knaus, William J. *Do It Now: Break the Procrastination Habit*. Rev. Ed. New York: J. Wiley, 1998.

Lively, Lynn. *The Procrastinator's Guide to Success*. New York: McGraw-Hill, 1999.

Newcombe, Jerry. *I'll Do It Tomorrow: How to Stop Putting It Off and Get It Done Today*. Illustrations by Johnny Hart. Nashville, TN: Broadman & Holman, 1999.

Peterson, Karen E. *The Tomorrow Trap: Unlocking the*

Secrets of the Procrastination-Protection Syndrome. Deerfield Beach, FL: Health Communications, 1996.

Porat, Frieda. *Creative Procrastination: Organizing Your Own Life.* 1st ed. San Francisco: Harper & Row, 1980.

Roberts, M. Susan. *Living Without Procrastination: How to Stop Postponing Your Life.* Oakland, CA: New Harbinger, 1995.

Sapadin, Linda. *It's About Time!: The Six Styles of Procrastination and How to Overcome Them.* New York, NY: Viking, 1996.

Sherman, James R. *Stop Procrastinating, Get To Work!* Los Altos, CA: Crisp Publications, 1989.

Tracy, Brian. *Eat That Frog!: 21 Great Ways to Stop Procrastinating and Get More Done in Less Time.* San Francisco, CA: Berrett-Koehler Publishers, 2001.

About this Author:

With no less than four respected industry certifications, Kerul is an internationally recognized professional coach, speaker, and teleclass leader. She is also the author of STOP PROCRASTINATING NOW, and the e-book AB$OLUTELY ATIFIED: *Mental Yoga for Growing Your Money Muscle$*. Kerul's internationally lauded programs such as *Anticrastinate Your Way to Success*, *Power De-cluttering for Busy People*, *Dissolving Writer's Block*, and *Get Ahead Without Getting a Headache* have been presented to major corporations nationwide.

Kerul is certified as a coach by the International Coach Federation, the International Association of Coaches, Coach U, and CoachVille, where she has served as Certifier, Senior Faculty Member, and Director of Personal Development Communities. She is a member of the International Coach Federation, National Speakers Association, National Association of Women Business Owners, and National Association of Professional Organizers.